*Para Joe KAPP
un Chicano
de huevos* — (handwritten signature)

11-3-93
SAn Jose CAlifornia — (handwritten)

Soldados:
Chicanos in Viet Nam

Edited by Charley Trujillo

**CHUSMA
HOUSE**

Chusma House Publications

This book is dedicated to:

Jose Barrera
Pedro Garcia
Julian Marin

Three soldiers from Corcoran who lost their lives
in Viet Nam.

Library of Congress Catalog Number: 89-81107
ISBN: 0-9624536-0-9

Book Design by Hiram Duran Alvarez
Typography by BookPrep, San Jose, California
Printed by Delta Lithograph Company, Valencia, California

second printing 1991

TABLE OF CONTENTS

PREFACE

When a reluctant group of wealthy aristocratic volunteers offered their services to the Roman general Publius Cornelius Scipio (later to become Scipio Africanus) before his invasion of Africa during the Second Punic War, he thanked them but suggested that perhaps they were averse to his military enterprise. He proceeded then to strip them of their expensively embellished armor and horses, and assigned the equiptment to more deserving men, many of whom were conscripts from the more wretched slums of Rome who ranked the legions of Rome's Imperial Army. The adage that the poor make more resolute and compliable soldiers is verified when applied to Chicanos. As the personal accounts in **Soldados: Chicanos in Viet Nam** attest, Chicanos were often the easiest and most malleable resource the U.S. had for achieving its quota for combat soldiers. And to those ends, they were used generously.

The personal accounts of these veterans, many of whom experienced the war viscerally and whose private reasons were myriad and expressed in this book with a severe authenticity, can be of service to all. They fought for reasons that were ill-defined, often confusing, but for the most part devoid of any cogent understanding of the political and economic forces at play which took them from labor fields in Corcoran, California, to rice paddies in Indochina. From their odyssey a

I

great house of knowledge can be gained, a knowledge that was, unfortunately, purchased with blood.

Viet Nam, to Chicanos, was the most questionable and dangerous undertaking of their lives. When drafted, they served, when "volunteered," they did so because of the scarcity of jobs and unequal opportunity of hope. Once there, they populated for the most part the trenches, and there were often maimed and killed. Many, incredibly enough, genuinely believed the propaganda of being "defenders of freedom" and went willingly. But most were victims of an economic exploitation and pernicious cultural suppression at home that made the military a step up in stature, and the need to "prove" oneself, a disturbing and misplaced search for self-esteem and acceptance as legitimate citizens. Of those who lived to return home, some were given medals to garnish the plate of their heroism, some were handed honorable discharges and the small gratuities of veteran's benefits. Others left Viet Nam with hidden deposits of agent orange waiting to erupt on the surface of their skin, and the ticking time bomb of post-traumatic stress disorder (PTSD). None left Viet Nam the same as when they entered.

But many questions continue to remain hidden and unexplored, and these hover ominously in the background of this book. How many Chicanos, for example, had the privilege of being exempt from service as opposed to the more prominent sectors of society? How many actually died or served closest to the more dangerous theaters of action? How many were predominately poor and working-class? These are questions that are just now being looked into, but most statistics are unavailable and when available, incomplete and, at times, anything but impartial. One study, for example, after concluding that of the 470,000 who suffer from PTSD, 27 percent are "Hispanic," suggested that the reasons for so swollen a figure was because many were raised in "unstable" families.

This poverty of information and its consequences, of

course, underscore the need for Chicano and Latino youth to attain a perspective as to where exactly they stand in relation to a society of which they are paradoxically both citizens and aliens. As a people grossly manipulated by factors over which they have little or no control, brutalized as a class and culture, Chicanos and Latinos must realize how pivotal and vitally significant their own attitudes and cultural allegiances are, and how important it is to their communities and to the country to be vocal about them. For them, Viet Nam is by no means over, and that is why Chicano Moratoriums continue every year in cities throughout the U.S. Chicano families, however "unstable," should be wary about again placing their youth in the line of sight of a gun barrel.

The accounts in this book also serve as a corrective reminder to many white North-Americans who are, for the most part, kept in a tragic state of unawareness as to how many Chicanos fought in the war, especially considering the almost total absence of Chicano soldiers in films, newspaper stories, television programs, and even war footage. That this book is the first of its kind, and issued so long after the fact, speaks much about the erasure of any conscious understanding of the war other than patriotic flag-waving. It is an erasure which persists despite our vaunted educational system and the impressive applause-tracks of our new Information Age.

In truth, the majority of people living in the U.S. know almost nothing about how our leaders perpetuated and instigated the Viet Nam war. Like Hiroshima, Viet Nam exhibited with scorching clarity the levels of arrogance and cruelty which the U.S. government can exert on any nation, anywhere in the world. Anything but a mistake, Viet Nam was a premeditated slaughter, and so it measured how much punishment we are willing to inflict on a people we held in contempt simply because they refused to benignly accept our superior dictates over their affairs. But in the absence of this assessment, Viet Nam to many, has become a long list of bogus rationales and self-serving justifications for spreading our own investments of state terrorism and death. The list runs so long that we grow tired of reading and close our eyes.

If there has been a prevalent notion promulgated by most major media sources and eloquent pundits on talk shows and lecture circuits, it is that Viet Nam was a "lesson," and this lesson is that "we" as a nation, should never again enter into a war unless "we" as a people are in consensus as to its objectives and are resolved to "win" it. There is also the popularly exchanged currency that our intentions were noble, our motives misguided but pure. History has shown these two astonishingly fashionable digressions to be somewhat effective but fraudulent placebos for recovering from what many national leaders diagnose as "The Vietnam Syndrome." Until the absurdity of Viet Nam became glaringly apparent, the U.S. public, whether outward proponents, or liberal columnists whose most pronounced criticism was a long and ineffectual whine, by and large supported the war by mass abstention.

Another misconception heard in the most acoustically resonant halls of free-market forums, is that Kennedy, Johnson, and later Nixon and Kissinger, skillfully "misled" the people of the U.S. through the media. This is not only unconscionably naive, but a slickly routed avoidance to divert culpability. The realities of Viet Nam were evident, and they should have seared a wound so deep into the body of America that a great and permanent scar would forever remind us of the crimes of which a materially gluttonous society such as ours is capable. A public that allows itself to be lied to by its leaders and misinformed by the institutions which should be providing it with honest information are not participants in a well-functioning democracy; they are conspirators, a curious ostrich of conspirators who think that if the knowledge of their acquiescence remains hidden, then they are innocent. Ignorance of this type ultimately creates a willful, self-induced amnesia couched in middle-class luxury which says much worse about us as a people than if we had accepted the ugly face of our belligerence from the beginning.

In the aftermath of Viet Nam, we in the U.S. need to quit making excuses and understand that it was our compliance, not solely the lies of our elected officials and not solely the complicit Fourth Estate, but our compliance, often mistaken for apathy, that helped perpetuate the ruthless, criminal lawlessness that went on in Viet Nam, and continues to go on in countries like El Salvador, Guatemala, Palestine, Haiti, Chile and South Africa. It is we who, in the end, brought a stop to the calculated ferocity called Viet Nam, and it is only we who can stop the others. That no excuses are justifiable and that perhaps no amount of atonement is possible should be prerequisite to this understanding. Until we recognize this, Viet Nam has not ended, no "lesson" has been learned, and we, as well as those we victimize at home and abroad, will always be susceptible to other and perhaps more deadly wars.

Victor Martinez

Victor Martinez is a writer and poet living in San Francisco.

INTRODUCTION

After reading many books on the soldier experience in the Viet Nam War, I noticed that Chicano soldiers are often glossed over. In fact we hardly exist; for example, in the national best seller, **Everything We Had** (Ballantine Books, 1982), not one Chicano is interviewed. Even in the book, **Bloods** (Ballantine Books, 1984), about blacks who fought in Viet Nam, Chicanos are rarely mentioned. Yet partial statistics gathered by the late Ralph Guzman from the University of California at Santa Cruz demonstrate that, while constituting ten percent of the population, twenty percent of the casualties for the five southwestern states of Arizona, Colorado, California, New Mexico and Texas were Spanish surnamed. Statistics on the exact number of Chicano casualties in the Viet Nam War are difficult to obtain because the Department of Defense did not count "Hispanics" until 1979. Before then, Chicanos and Latinos were classified as "white." However, the Department of Defense has estimated that 83,000 Hispanics served in Viet Nam. Viet Nam veterans' advocate Ruben Treviso writes in the book, **Vietnam Reconsidered** (Harper and Row, 1984), that twenty percent of Latinos that went to Viet Nam were killed and thirty-three percent were wounded. This group was also disproportionately drafted in accordance to their representation in the population. From Guzman's and Treviso's figures and my own research, there is more than a strong suggestion that Chicanos throughout the nation fought and died in disproportionate numbers in Viet Nam.

I decided, as a consequence of this lack of literature, to conduct reserch and document the war experiences of those Chicanos of my hometown of Corcoran, an agriculturally based community of 6,000 (thirty percent of whom are Chicanos) situated in the Central San Joaquin Valley of California. Unfortunately, this leaves out Chicanos from other parts of the nation; yet, I feel these narratives could have been given by Chicanos from such places as Raton, New Mexico, Greely, Colorado; as well as barrios in Tucson, Arizona; San Antonio, Texas; and Chicago. I should also add that there were soldados who were born in Tijuana, Mexicali, Piedras Negras and many other places from Mexico who served in Viet Nam—green cards and all.

From my observations during my military stint in Viet Nam, regardless of where they were from, Chicanos were united by a common culture and history. Two limits of this book are the lack of Chicano officers and Chicana Viet Nam Veterans, who I know exist but whom I could not locate in Corcoran.

The veterans interviewed in this book are often related, friends, neighbors, schoolmates, or sometimes even enemies. One veteran was born in Mexico, a few were born in Texas but most were born in Corcoran or Hanford, California. The majority of the veterans are from families that have been in the United States for generations. Some can trace their families to a time when the southwest was Mexico. Many veterans' uncles and fathers served in World War II and the Koren War.

The accounts given by the veterans are honest and candid. Details of many incidents given in the text are ones that other books in this area either ignore or downplay. Miguel Gastelo and Guillermo Alvidrez describe the defeat of the US Army on the battlefield. Gastelo details the sophisticated military tactics used by the North Vietnamese. Placed within a historical perspective, Alvidrez's account in terms of casualties rivals the defeat of General George Custer at Little Big Horn—about two hundred and fifty men killed. Larry Holguin, David Delgado, Diego Garcia, and Ramon Rosas disclose their problems with military justice "Heroism and the stockade" as Jose Montoya writes in the poem "El Louie." Miguel Lemus reveals the killing of an army captain by his own troops. Richard Holguin divulges the actual sighting of "Salt and Pepper," two marines who according to soldier lore went over to the North Vietnamese side. Mike Solis, after two tours of Viet Nam and several wounds, leaves the army disillusioned. The same holds for Herbert De La Fuente who repeatedly goes AWOL after his return from Viet Nam. Manuel Marin tells of the devastating effect of his brother's death in Viet Nam. Ernest explains that the only morale the soldiers had in Viet Nam was a group of soldiers bound together for the sole purpose of staying alive. Freddie Cavasos begins to question the war but is directly hit by an artillery round before he can fully comprehend the war. Frank Delgado realizes how the war had transformed his morality and how he felt used by the military. My own account is about a mutiny I participated in.

I have translated some of the text from Spanish to English but have left some Spanish words and phrases whenever possible in order for the reader to get a sense of Chicano speech. Translatoins are provided at the end of the book. I have also kept much of the language intact because I belive authentic language best captures reality. It is the hope of the editor, without being didactic, that this book will show war es a very seious undertaking in terms of human suffering and distruction, and that it not romanticize or glorify the Viet Nam experience as much of the current lituratue seems to do.

The reason I have started Chusma House is because publishers refused to accept my manuscript. I was able to have several major publishing companies review parts of my manuscript but was turned down by all of them. The most interesting rejections came from companies that have published oral history books of the soldier experience in Viet Nam. I wrote to them explaining that I felt my manuscript would fit nicely within their current list of books on white soldiers, black soldiers, women, POW's and the general soldiers experience. I feel these rejections are a reflection of this society's lack of appreciation of the blood and sacrifices given by Chicanos in serving the United States.

The reasons, or rather excuses, for the rejections were along the lines of, "We don't think the public would like to read what your book has to say." My answer to this is that it is the publisher who does not want the public to read this book. Another standard excuse, "There already is too much of that published." I was told that two years ago and since then there has been a plethora of books written about the soldier experience in the Viet Nam War and I am sure there will be others.

Some publishers were even genuinely surprised that we don't dress like Speedy Gonzales, ride around on donkeys and that we speak English. In other words, just plain ignorance and stereotypical thinking. The media has historically depicted Chicanos in a very negative light. Conversely, at the present time Chicanos in the media attempt to offset this by depicting Chicanos in a very positive light. The position of Chusma House is to neither depict Chicanos negatively or positively, but rather to write about them honestly, realistically, and unpretensiously.

Though the focus of Chusma House will be on Chicanos, other racial and ethnic groups will be included in the writings. You will notice that in Soldados other ethnic and racial groups are dealt with in many aspects. Paradoxically, racial solidarity as well as racial conflict is disclosed.

It is the conviction of Chusma House that literature is about the human experience and is universal, and it is time for

Chicanos to be included in this universe of literature on our own cultural and political terms. We cannot rely on the established publishers, who for the most part are ideologically and economically bound to the status quo, to produce a progressive body of Chicano literature. With this in mind, there are other books in the planning stages.

I would like to thank all the veterans who cooperated especially Miguel Gastelo and Diego Garcia. I would also like to thank Tina Alvarez-Robles, Juan Felipe Hererra, Guillermo Hernandez, Ramon Lerma, Guy McFarland, Victor Martinez, Hilda Peinado, Mary Shoane and Margarita Luna Robles for their editorial assistance and encouragement. Also Ramona Castellanos, Gilbert Garza, Fred Johnson Jr., Connie Vega, Renaldo and Gloria Carboni, Roberto and Hilda De Anda, Fred and Petra Escallante, Ramon and Lola Lerma, and my parents Ramon and Maria Guadalupe for their financial and moral support. Special thanks go to Isabell Molano for her patience and hard work in typing the manuscript and Hiram Alvarez for the art work. I am also greatful to Benny Barco, Tommy Castillo, Pedro Gomez and Joe Orosco for their special assistance in providing information from their Viet Nam experiences.

TEENAGE SOLDIER

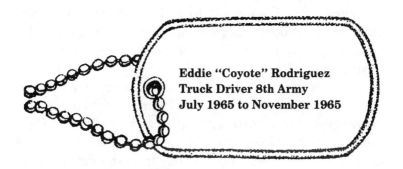

Eddie "Coyote" Rodriguez
Truck Driver 8th Army
July 1965 to November 1965

M e and some of the guys went to see the selective service before we graduated from high school. They told us that they would give us two years in the army if we volunteered for the draft. We wanted to go into the army for several reasons. We wanted to get it over with. We couldn't or didn't have the grades to go to college. I knew that once I got out of school I was probable going to end working in the fields. That's all there was to do in Corcoran. My father told me not to be dumb and to go to the army in order to get some sort of training or else I was going to work out in the fields like my other brothers and four sisters I am the only one who finished high school. So, I volunteered for the draft.

As soon as we graduated, the selective service called us in. But I didn't get to go because I got in trouble. I was messing around with some of the guys and I ended up in jail for thirty days. After I got out of jail, they let me volunteer for the draft

1

three months later. We were picking prunes in San Jose, California, when I got my draft notice in 1963.

I was taken to Oakland California, for processing. And by the next morning, I was in Fort Ord. "Get up, God damnit, you're in the army." At first I was scared. I thought, *"Estan cabrones estos vatos aqui."*

Two weeks after I got in the army they killed Kennedy. I thought we were really in for it then. They took us out to the parade field and they stood the whole Fort Ord in formation for seven hours. We stood there and nobody knew what was going on: everybody was going nuts. People were going this way, people were going that way, and nobody was saying anything.

At first they had us at attention for about an hour, then they put us at ease for about fifteen minutes, then they put us at attention for another hour. This went on for the whole fucking day. I think there must've been about thirty thousand guys there. There were guys fainting from standing at attention too long. They finally let us go back to the barracks and the following day we did the same thing again. At first I thought it was done to honor Kennedy, but after awhile I didn't know why we were doing it (standing in the parade field). We had just gotten to basic training ... we didn't even know how to march yet. We looked like a bunch of sloppy soldiers because the uniforms they gave us didn't fit right. We looked like a bunch of dodos ... *todos pelones, todos hasta la chingada.*

After I finished basic training I was assigned to Fort Ord for truck driving school. The rest of the guys were sent to other places around the country. I wanted to go to another place too, but I was stuck in Fort Ord. And after I finished the school, I still had to stay in Fort Ord as a truck driver.

But my being in Fort Ord was all right too because I was close to Corcoran and San Jose where my brothers and parents lived.

They were always giving me different jobs at Fort Ord ...

porque estaba muy chavalon y me importaba pito. They'd fire me from one assignment and then give me another one. Since I worked in the motor pool, I always got driving jobs. One of the jobs that they gave me was driving a brigadier general around. I didn't last very long at that job because the *vato* (general) would get mad at me. I hated that job because you always had to be in proper uniform and salute officers in other vehicles.

In July of 1965, our unit was transferred to Viet Nam ... we took all the trucks and jeeps to Oakland where they were loaded on ships. It took us about a month to take all the vehicles that we had.

We were given a two-week leave before we were sent to Viet Nam. We were put on this big boat. It must've held about two thousand troops. We got to eat once a day—that was because they had so many soldiers to feed. But when you got to eat, you could eat all you wanted.

The quarters were really cramped ... there was barely enough room to walk sideways and ship's sleeping quarters. Guys were sick on the ship all of the time. It was a mess because a lot of guys were throwing up all over the place, and we were always mopping the puke up. I got sick the first few days, but some guys were sick all the way to Viet Nam. We'd play a lot of cards, and some of the guys would play guitars and sing. It took twenty-two days to get to Nam. About the only thing I was worried about on the ship was that it might sink, and I didn't know how to swim.

After about eighteen days they let us get off the boat in Guam. That island is beautiful. They took us to the beach on trucks, gave us a barbecue and lots of beer, and everybody got real drunk. All of the *raza* got together and partied. Some of the guys played guitars, and we had a good time. I think one of the reasons they let us off was so that the boat could be washed down, it was so full of puke. There were a few guys that went nuts before we got to Nam. They put them in strait jackets ... everything was too cramped and closed in.

3

Soldados

We landed off the coast of Qui Nhon, Viet Nam. They loaded us off the boat in barges. We stayed there on the beach for a couple of days. There was a lot of activity not to mention soldiers going back and forth. All during this time we were not fired upon. From the beach, we were marched out about two miles inland where we began to build our base camp. At that time we were attached to the First Cavalry Division.

Once we got there, we didn't have to worry about physical hygiene, like shaving, hair cuts, and clean uniforms. I never did get to shoot at anybody, but we always carried our M-14 rifles. We had troops in the hills guarding us. A few times we did get mortared, but they were mostly trying to knock out the trucks. When they did that, those mortar positions were knocked out within a matter of hours.

My first assignment was to carry troops from the barges to different base camps. I had a five-ton cattle truck that carried about 100 troops. I transported a lot of different troops: Australians, Koreans, Americans and Indians. One time, I was carrying some Korean soldiers, when they called the ROK Army, and when it came time to disconnect the trailer, their captain told them to help disconnect it. It had a handle which was really easy to turn. I knew how to do it with one hand, but they were little guys and they couldn't do it. There were about five or four of them that tried. When they couldn't do it, their captain came over and began to hit them with a stick. I thought, poor guys, they treat them like dogs. I'd sure hate to be in their army. Those guys looked so weak that it seemed you could just push them and they'd fall down. The Australians were big assholes. Now those Indians were big motherfuckers. I never seen so many big sons-of-a-bitches in one place at a time. They were black and they wore those white ropes around their heads.

After a couple of months there, we got Vietnamese to come in to make trenches and dig holes for bathrooms. Then we got girls to come in and clean up the tents we lived in. They'd shine all the shoes, make our beds, wash our clothes, and work in the kitchen washing dishes. All we did was drive. We had it good.

Soon afterwards, the Vietnamese built these little bars out of cardboard and tin cans. Most of the time we didn't even have to go to town to party because they were right there. They'd sell you anything . . . they built little whorehouses real quick.

We were partying in one of those bars one time and talking to some girls. There was one Vietnamese there that had a bullet hole in his shoulder. I think the son-of-a-bitch was a Viet Cong. He was just sitting there and looking at us real kind of funny like. All of this time we were playing around with Vietnamese girls who just wanted our money. I grabbed the head of one of the girls and shook it. She was full of lice and they fell all over the table. So me and my buddy took our forty-fives out and began to kill them with the handles. The Vietnamese got a big kick out of this.

I asked the wounded Vietnamese, "Who shot you?" "Oh, VC, VC shot me," he said. "Bullshit, I bet you the Americans shot your fucking ass, didn't they, motherfucker. Go fucking around there again you fucking asshole," I told him. He just kept saying, "No, no, VC shot me." "Bullshit," I told him. "Just keep coming around my yard again, and I'm going to shoot you right between the eyeballs, *cabron.*" I was just fucking with him, and we bought him a beer anyway.

They used to send us to the garbage dump to get rid of all the trash and the whole dump was full of people. Those people would come in and take everything: beer cans, cardboard, food . . . whatever was there. That whole dump looked clean. Those people were like human buzzards. When we were there, we'd throw cans of C-rations to the sides and kids would scramble to get them, then we would throw another to the other side until we had them going every which way. Some of the guys would put C-ration cans in the middle of the barbed wire around our perimeter. The kids would crawl between the wire to get the cans, and they would scratch the hell out of themselves. I wouldn't do that, but some sadistic *gabachos* would do it. I saw this kid yelling his head off in the middle of the wire, but he didn't give up until he got the can... he was all cut up. At first, I felt bad about those poor people, but afterwards I didn't give a shit anymore. I just got used to it.

Early in the morning when we'd start out on our runs, there would be a lot of Vietnamese carrying their goods to market. They wouldn't get off the damn road and our orders were for us not to stop. We would honk our horns to try and get them to move out of the way. But they wouldn't move because they were trying to make us stop, and that's dangerous because that's when you could get a grenade thrown at you. There were quite a few guys that got killed like that. After awhile they told us that if we hit somebody we were not to worry about it and just keep on going. We had to do it. I wasn't trying to get off the road and hit them on purpose. You'd see these older people, who were laying on the side of the road who couldn't even make it to market. The other people would walk right over them—they wouldn't pick them up or anything, poor people.

I thought I was going to get it sooner or later. A lot of guys were getting killed by mines and snipers. One of my good friends, Alvarez, was killed by a mine. He was only about two or three trucks ahead of me. When this happened, everybody pulled over quick, then we began to move again. We just went around the burning truck. I don't know what ever happened to Alvarez' body because we just left him there.

Sometimes, I would go to the base camp of the infantry units. They would have a bunch of bodies lined up. You could tell the ones who were Americans and the ones who were Vietnamese because the Americans were covered with ponchos. The Viet Cong weren't covered with anything and were thrown together like in a big ball. I'm glad I never got picked to transport dead bodies. I'd take anything else, but I wouldn't pick up dead bodies.

Eddie Rodriguez

I was talking to some of the chopper gunners once, and they told me that they had just captured a couple of VC's who they took up on the chopper. But when they didn't want to give any information, they would drop one out. When they brought the other one down, they couldn't make that guy stop talking. They were doing all kinds of shit out there. A lot of those guys were fucking nuts. They were just a bunch of punk kids trying to prove that they were bad. They were just a bunch of assholes.

I weighed 145 pounds when I got to Viet Nam and I weighed 115 pounds when I left. It was real hot over there. And when the monsoon season came, it was just as hot except that it would begin to rain all of a sudden . . . it would seem that we began to smoke when the rain hit us.

Our company commander had already been to Viet Nam before, so he already knew what to expect when we got there. He had been a Green Beret. He was a pretty good guy. Out of the whole company, I was the youngest one because I had volunteered. I was a fuck up a lot of the time. I was a private most of the time and only corporals could have their own trucks, but the captain would let me have my own truck because I was a good worker and driver. I made corporal but I only kept it for a couple of days because I was partying and didn't get back when I was supposed to. I didn't care about stuff like that, fuck it. At that time I really didn't care. I was eighteen and I was having a ball.

We were carrying supplies from Qui Nhon to Pleiku one afternoon when my truck went out near Able mountain. We were going up the mountain when the truck flooded out. I thought it had run out of gas or that the lines had been mixed up from one tank to another. The convoy couldn't wait for me because it was getting late. So they told me that I was going to have to stay by myself and that they would come back for me. They left me there, and I began to work on my truck. But I coudln't get that son–of–a–bitch started for nothing. Then a jeep came for me. Some officer in the jeep asked if I

7

couldn't get it started. He tried to start it, but all he was doing was running the battery low. I told him to leave it alone because he was going to mess up my battery. "All right" he said, "but we'll be back."

It was already getting dark when I decided to check the gas filter. I removed the filter, cleaned it, and put it back. Then I let the filter fill with gas . . . it started. By this time, it was dusk, and I started up the mountain. Two jeeps and a tow truck were coming down the mountain. All this time I was scared, I thought, "Oh! shit the VC are going to catch me alone now that it is dark."

I made it without a scratch. I thought everybody was going to know that I was coming home. When I got home, nobody even knew I had gotten home. Nobody even knew I was gone in the first place. I was expecting a band to be waiting for me. The only ones who really knew I had left was my family.

THE ANTS

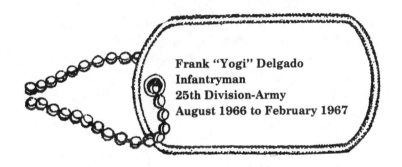

Frank "Yogi" Delgado
Infantryman
25th Division-Army
August 1966 to February 1967

On TV and in the movies you always see the Viet Nam *veteranos* being portrayed as being deranged or crazy . . . I don't think that's right. There was a lot of stuff going on over there . . . people were getting loaded. I was there in 1966, and back then there wasn't any heroin in Nam. That came about later on. Which I'm glad about because who's to say that being only ninteen and foolish, maybe I would have tried it or maybe I wouldn't have. I really don't know. Now I realize that I was immature. I see a nineteen year old kid today and I say to myself, was I that foolish? I can't see a nineteen year old kid fighting a war.

When we were in high school in Corcoran—Corcoran, a little bitty hick town—a couple of the buddies and me would round up some money and go way out in the country with a six pack and drink two or three beers. We didn't have to go way out there, like if someone was going to be looking for us. In those days, we never even thought about grass and all that.

9

Because back in 1965, that was synonymous with somebody who had already been to prison and all of that. I graduated from high school in June, 1965, and by February, 1966, I was drafted into the army.

I was driving barley harvesters when I was drafted. In our family, all the boys worked but the girls never did. They would help my mom, which is plenty of work, I found out about this later. It's twice as much work as a nine to five job. Being from Corcoran, you kind of hate to leave the place, but you kind of look forward to it, too. Hey, it's like you're ready for something else, there's got to be something better. I had mixed feelings about going into the army. The opportunities in Corcoran were very limited. I accepted it, and I didn't try to fight it or anything. I had the attitude of taking everything on a day to day basis, one day at a time, in other words. That seemed to work for me.

In our house, we all worked as a family, and my jefita would get all the checks, and she would pay all of the bills. Then she would give us what she thought we needed, usually a couple of dollars here and there. She would buy all the clothes and other stuff that we needed. I was just used to handing all the money over to her. I remember when I got my first pay-check from the army, I sent fifty dollars out of the seventy-five dollars that I got paid to my mom because I was used to doing that. I had never had seventy-five dollars in my whole life.

I knew a lot of people who, once they got out of school, would move here and there. I had really never been anywhere to speak of. That's probably why I kind of had an open mind. I always had the feeling that no matter what happened, I was going to survive. I was going to pull through. I had confidence that God was going to see me through it.

I went to basic training in Fort Ord, California. I knew about Fort Ord from Quelo and Eddie Coyote who would go down to Corcoran for the weekend from Fort Ord. They'd come down with their uniforms on and I'd see them in the dances. To me, they looked sharp with their khaki uniforms on. I used to think to myself, "Hey! That ain't too bad, you're in Fort Ord and get to come home on the weekends and throw parties with your uniform on." I didn't think that was too bad. It's not too shabby. But when I got to Fort Ord, the place was in quarantine, which meant that you didn't come out until you finished your basic training. Fort Ord was under quarantine because of spinal meningitis. Before that, a lot of people would go home after three or four weeks on weekend passes. I don't know why they wouldn't even let us leave the company area.

After we had been in the fourth week of basic, they finally let us go to the PX and drink some booze. We got five minutes to drink all the booze we could. We were there like *mensos* drinking away. I remember the sergeant went squad by squad, telling us when we could go in and buy the beer. Only the squad leader could go in and buy the beer. The sergeant would ask, "First squad, how many beers do you want?" "We want two six packs, drill sergeant," they would answer. "How many six packs do you want, second squad?" "We want three six-packs, drill sergeant!" they would answer. "Fourth squad, how many six packs do you want?" They wanted something like seven six packs. "Hey!" the sergeant said. "You got all the drunks in your squad."

In the fifth week of basic, every thing came down. Then they said, "Well now, we are going to give you guys a chance to drink all the beer you want. We're going to have like a little outing." It wasn't really a picnic because all we mostly had was beer in those big-old-ice-chest-OD-cannisters. Then they told us that we were going to celebrate Easter. In order to make it more interesting, they were going to read the orders for everybody's next assignments. Everybody was all for it. Me and Frank Molano were the only Chicanos from Corcoran in our company. When they read Frank's orders it was kind of unusual because he was to take his advanced training in Panama. Other guys were being sent to different places, but the place you didn't want to go was Fort Polk, Louisiana,

"Tiger-Land," because that meant you were going to Nam—
that's it. Then the sergeant said that they were going to name
the people who were going to be sent to Fort Polk. *Hijola man,*
I thought. I hoped I wouldn't get Fort Polk because I knew
that Fort Polk meant Nam. The first name that they read out
was mine. I hadn't even had a beer yet. That's when Frank told
me that we should go drink some more. I told him that I didn't
feel like drinking because I knew what was going to go on in
Viet Nam.

I still had the attitude of taking whatever comes, but you
don't want to ask for it.

I got a two week leave before I went to Fort Polk. When it
was time to report to Fort Polk, my *jefitos* dropped me off at
the Visalia Airport. It was quite an experience for my parents
because they really aged a lot when I went into the army.
Especially when I went to Nam and then my *carnal* Steve
went too. From Visalia I flew to LA and from there I flew to
Dallas, and from Dallas to Houston on a little beat-up plane. It
was really hot because this was the summer of 1966. I was
sitting there looking out the window when I saw this bus
parked in the parking lot. The bus driver was a *mayate,* the
teacher was a *mayate,* all of the students were *mayates.* I was
not used to seeing that because in Corcoran, Okies, *mayates*
and Chicanos all go to school together. That's when I started
realizing how confined and sheltered we were in Corcoran.
That's the first time in my life that I had ever seen segregation. I really couldn't believe it because the Civil Rights Act
was passed in 1964 and this was 1966. In Corcoran there was
some segregation, but it was more like behind your back.

I was real green back then. My orders said that I was
supposed to be in Fort Polk on such and such a date, but I
didn't realize that you had a twenty-four hour grace period. If
your orders say to be there the 15th, you really don't have to
be there until the 16th. Well, I got there the day they said. Me
and this other *menso* Mexican were the only ones who were
there on time.

Fort Ord was just like what they call it, "basic training." But Advanced Individual Training (AIT) in Fort Polk was entirely different. There was no time to mess around. The nickname that Fort Polk had, "Tiger-Land," was synonymous with a tiger which is real strong and nothing can beat it. Fort Polk was real good training. They literally brainwashed you.

When I first got to Fort Polk, this Chicano sergeant Carmona, who had been with the First Cav in Nam and had a scar across his forehead as a reminder, told me, "Well, I want you to know right now that in nine weeks you're going to go to Nam." I knew it already because Fort Polk meant Nam. All of the cadre were Viet Nam veterans.

The town closest to Fort Polk was Leesville. It was about the size of Corcoran. We used to call it fleasville or disease-ville. Louisiana is as bad as Alabama when it comes to segregation. We went to Leesville one time, and it was me, a *gabacho* Jimmy Smith, and this *mayate* went to this restaurant to eat. We were in our khaki uniforms and we were waiting to be served. We waited for awhile, and then we noticed other people were being served and waited on. Finally I asked this fat, redneck waitress, "Hey! When are you going to take my order?" She looked at us and said, "Hey! We don't serve niggers here." I have never been a person to go around fighting. I think I have only been in a couple of fights in my whole life. But I got mad in this situation and so did the *gabacho*. I felt that I had to do something. That's when the *mayate* said, "Naw man, just look around you." We looked at the bar and there were about ten rednecks looking at us—just staring at us. The best thing to do in that situation, which we did, was get up and leave. What are you going to do? I'll never forget that incident. The war had been going on for two years already and we were in our army uniforms trying to get a meal. And they pull that shit on us?

All this time I still had the attitude, I'll take one day at a time, and somehow I knew I would make it. But I wasn't going to go ask for it. I wasn't going to join airborne. I wasn't going to volunteer for the infantry. I had a lot of *camaradas* that did and that's fine, but that wasn't for me. I didn't volunteer for infantry, but that's what I got.

Slowly and slowly they started pumping you full of shit, that's what it really amounts to. They were building you up and telling you how good you're doing. Then they started giving you passes and telling us, "You're a big man now. You can go out on your own. You can drink beer and go out."

When you're already a soldier in Tiger-Land, you get to go to what they called Piece-On-Ridge. Piece-On-Ridge is where you get one week of bivouac. After about the third or fourth day of eating C-rations and living out in the mountains, you feel like "Hey, man I can do it." A day before we were going to go back to Fort Polk, the sergeant told us that so many units had already gone through there and that we were the best ones, and everybody believed him. His thing was that, "Yea, I know I can send you to Nam and that a year from now you will still be doing your shit out in the street." We were so worked up that we were literally looking forward to going to Nam. We wanted to go to Nam.

When I got my orders for Nam, I knew that I was going to be in the 25th Infantry Division. As soon as I found out what unit I was being assigned to, I went out and bought some 25th Division patches. Other guys bought the patches for the other divisions that they were being assigned to. At this time they gave us two weeks leave.

When I went into the army I weighed 191 pounds and when I came out of Tiger-Land, I weighed 160 pounds. I was lean and ready to go to Nam. I was psyched up and thought that nothing could hurt us. We were the best. We were infantry, and we had all that good training. I have to admit that the training we got in Fort Polk was damned good. We were ready, both physically and mentally about as fit as you can be at nineteen years old. I didn't know what to expect.

It took me three days to get home from Fort Polk because

there was an airline strike. Some of the guys and I rented a car and I got off at El Paso. I took a flight from El Paso to LA. When I got to LA, I told them I wanted a flight to Visalia. It was about ten o'clock at night and they told me the last flight had just left. And, there wasn't another flight until seven in the morning. I got a cab and I went to the bus depot. I caught a bus from LA to Bakersfield. I was falling asleep on the bus when it stopped in West Hollywood. Some guy with a white jacket got on the bus. "Hey, can I sit here?" he said. "Yeah, go ahead," I told him. I didn't think nothing of it even though there were a bunch of empty seats. I was falling asleep when I feel this guy feeling my leg. As soon as I felt that, I   elbowed him."Man get the hell out of here," I told him. I was kind of like shocked, more scared than anything else.

I finally got to Corcoran at about six in the morning on a Tuesday. I called my *jefitos* up from Bakersfield at about one in the morning. I told them that I would be in Tulare at five in the morning. But my mom and dad got up right away and got dressed, and they went off to Tulare to wait for me.

I was kind of anxious to get home because I had gotten a trophy in AIT. I wanted to show everybody in my family the trophy that I had gotten because I had scored the highest in the proficiency test. I felt real proud. When I got to the Greyhound Station in Bakersfield, there wasn't another bus going to Tulare until seven in the morning. They told me to go across the street and ask at the Continental Trailways Station if they had anything going south. they told me they had one, but they didn't know if it stopped in Tulare. That's when the bus pulled in and they told me to go ask the bus driver if he would leave me there. When I asked him if he stopped in Tulare, he told me they didn't. "Hey, man, you know what? I've been on the road for three days, and I've got two weeks before I have to go to Nam." He wasn't supposed to stop in Tulare at all, but he left me at the Chevron gas station on Airport Avenue 200. Every time I go by there I remember that time.

I got a taxi to where my parents were waiting for me. When I got home my brother Steve was on leave before he was to go to AIT. I was having a good time while I was on leave, eating good and partying.

Before I knew it, my day had come to report to Oakland Army Terminal on August the seventh, nineteen sixty-six.

We flew from Travis Air Force Base to Viet Nam with a stopover in Hawaii and the Philippines. The airport in Hawaii is real pretty, with the ocean and the breeze, the whole works. I thought to myself about what I had to go through in order to see a place like this. People who are well off can fly over there easily. But I couldn't understand why I had the chance to stop in Hawaii under these circumstances.

I was thinking about going AWOL there. But I thought, what am I going to do? Call up my mom and tell her to send me some money because I'm going to go AWOL? Just as much as she didn't want me to go to Nam, I think she would have worried just as much with me being AWOL. Besides, I think we had it better than the soldiers in WWII. In Viet Nam, the enemy did not have bombs and airplanes to attack us like in WWII. They didn't have R&R, and when they were killed, they were buried overseas, whereas the solders killed in Viet Nam were sent home to their parents for a funeral.

As we were getting off the plane at Ton Son Nhut Airport, other soldiers were going to take the same plane home to the States. There was this little, short *mayate* going up the stairs of the plane. He was drunker than a skunk. He was singing the Stevie Wonder song, *Uptight.* It was all right for him because he was going back home. That's when it really sunk in that I had a whole year to go over there. As we got off, we could see all sorts of flashes and bombs going off in the mountains. This was about two in the morning.

In AIT they trained us good. But in a way, they didn't

train us good enough because all they told us was the VC this and the VC that. So I thought that we were just going to be fighting the VC. I had no idea about the North Vietnamese Army. Every time they would show us the VC they would be in black pajamas and cone-head straw hats. To me, anyone who wore that was a VC. They took us on a bus through Saigon on our way to Camp Alpha, and what were ninety percent of the people wearing? Black pajamas and straw hats. I thought to myself, *Hijola man!* The VC are all around us.

We finally got to Camp Alpha where they assigned us to tents. The first night I was in Nam there was shooting all night along the perimeter. It was especially frightening because we hadn't been issued any weapons. Finally the next morning came and we found out what all the noise was about. Every time that the guards would hear noise along the perimeter, they would start shooting. In the morning there were a bunch of monkeys caught on the wire, all shot up and dead. They made the mistake of tripping tripflare wires.

After two or three days, I was sent to Pleiku. I was assigned to headquarters company. I thought that was pretty good. When they were giving out the assignments they asked us if anyone knew how to play a musical instrument, or type. The guys that did were assigned as clerks or to the band, which was real good duty. I was put in a reconnaissance platoon.

From Pleiku I was sent to my unit which was out in the I Drang Valley. I was assigned to my squad and when night came, and we found out what all the noise was about. Every and deeper. Sergeant Lowry and a *gabacho* they called the colonel were together in the same position. Sergeant Lowry took the first watch, the colonel the second, and me the third. I had always thought that soldiers slept in foxholes, but we didn't. We would sleep behind the foxhole. We only got into them when we received fire. A little after I had laid down I began to smell something funny, something I hadn't ever smelled before. It was the sergeant and the colonel smoking grass. "Hey, you want some?" they asked me. "No, man," I told them.

Somehow I fell asleep. I don't know how I did it because I was so scared. For some reason I woke up at about two or three in the morning. I sat up and looked around and the sergeant and the colonel had gotten so loaded that they had gone and visited their friends and left me there asleep. Man! That really freaked me out. I didn't know what to think. I got my M-16 and jumped into the foxhole. All that was in my head was the VC. Did the VC come and take these guys without seeing me? The position next to me was about twenty yards away and I couldn't see them. I started looking to the front and I couldn't see nothing. The moon was hitting the treeline ahead of me and then the wind started blowing. Pretty soon I actually started hallucinating, I could see people with rifles coming at me. I think now that God must've been with me because I actually pulled the trigger and my rifle wouldn't go off. It was good that it didn't go off because I would have made a bunch of noise and attracted attention to myself. It was bad that it jammed because if I had actually needed it, it wouldn't have gone off.

Pretty soon I hear some noises, and here come the sergeant and the colonel. Oh! Lord, they were laughing. They were just having a blast. I was glad to see the next morning. This went on for a long time until I finally got used to it. Out in the field I never got loaded because I was so pumped up from being out there.

Everyday the lieutenant would give us the information that intelligence had given him. He would tell us where they thought the enemy was and that their morale was low. Now, how in the hell did intelligence know that their morale was low? Did they go out and take a survey or what? But at nineteen years old, we thought, they don't call them intelligence for nothing.

We did a lot of humping out in the Central Highlands. Those were mountains out there, not hills. It was about 120°

in the day time and 50° at night. It was a hell of a drop. That was in the dry season, which wasn't too bad, but when the monsoon came, it came down. It would just rain and rain and rain.

About two or three weeks after I got to Nam, we were out on an observation post (OP), Sergeant Lowry, the *marijuano,* was with us. We were kind of like following him. Pretty soon Sergeant Lowry does a double take and gets on his stomach and starts firing. "They're over there. There are seven of them," he said. I looked over there and I couldn't see nothing. All I could see was just bush. I began to fire too. I was firing in the direction that Sergeant Lowry was. Pretty soon he stopped firing. So, me and the rest of the squad stopped too. When the rest of the platoon came to where we were at, hey, I still didn't see nobody. We didn't know what had happened. So, the whole platoon got on line and we threw a sweep down the mountain. We were shooting about fifty yards away. We went down slowly. *Hijola! Man!* I was just getting deeper and deeper into it, still keeping this positive attitude. As we were getting closer, I didn't know what was going to happen. That's when I stepped on a dead North Vietnamese soldier. That guy had been laying out in the sun for three or four days. The guy was bloated and purple all over, and the ants were eating out his eyes. His hair was stiff like straw. Man! That scared the hell out of me. When I looked down, I looked right into his face.

Later we figured out what happened. There had been a fire fight a week before and the North Vietnamese were trying to retrieve their dead. The reason they wanted to pick up their dead was because they believe that if you leave a dead person behind, that person will come back and haunt you for the rest of your life. They would even leave the wounded before they would a dead person.

I was lucky in that all of the time I was there we only ran into small parties of North Vietnamese. Some of the guys who been there longer than I had used to throw party on them. The first month I was there I didn't have any jungle boots. All I had was regular combat boots and I was slipping and falling all over the place.

On September 9th, exactly one month after I had gotten to Nam, we were given an assignment to check out a North Vietnamese camp. We had the coordinates and we found the camp about 11 a.m., but they weren't there. So we thought we would be slick and wait until they came back and ambush them. It started raining and pretty soon we started hearing howitzers going off over our heads. In training they had told us that as long as you heard the whistling sound it's no problem. It's when it stops whistling that it is going to hit where you're at. That's when I heard the whistling sound. Then it stopped and before I could hit the ground that thing went off. There was shit flying everywhere . . . limbs, trees, rocks, and all kinds of stuff.

Somebody must've messed up because it was our own artillery that was firing at us. I was on the ground when this *mayate,* Washington, kept grabbing me on my arm. "Hey! what's wrong with you," I told him. "You're hit on your arm," he said. I raised up my arm and blood was coming out of my sleeve. When I saw that, boom, the pain hit me. My arm became real heavy and it was burning and I could feel the shrapnel. The lieutenant called in and the firing finally stopped. I looked around and I knew I was lucky to be alive. The butt of my rifle was completely blown off, the bullets in the magazine were literally twisted. The gun was useless.

After the artillery stopped, they called in a dust-off and I was taken to a field hospital. Of the ten guys, I was the only one hit. When I got there they took care of the guys who were worse off than me first. I remember seeing all these guys on stretchers. They were all dead. There must've been ten to fifteen dead. Two guys would come, pick them up and take them inside a tent. I guess they were taking their guts out and stuff because I could hear them working away on them inside the tent. I went up and looked at the dead guys to see if I knew any of them. I didn't.

When they saw my wound, they didn't think it was that bad compared to other wounds. From the field hospital, I was sent to Pleiku which was about eight hours after I had been wounded. I still hadn't received any medical attention. They finally operated on me and removed a two inch piece of shrapnel. From there I was taken to the hospital in Qui Nhon.

When I got there, I had a big old bandage on my arm. It had dried up and gotten into the wound. He (doctor) said he wanted to see it, so what he did was just grab the bandage, pulled on it hard and took it off. Right about that time everything got real bright, like when somebody flashes a camera in your face. Then the doctor asked me, "Are you all right?" I'm still trying to be tough and answered, "Yea." There was an old nurse there, I don't even know why she was there because she was that old. She would call me sonny. She told the doctor that he shouldn't have done that. By then my arm was just bleeding. Then the doctor looked at my wound. He told me that it had a lot of debris and that somebody had done a poor job of cleaning it out. It had gotten infected.

After I left the doctor, I began to walk to a tent to lie down. As I was walking, everything started getting whiter and whiter and whiter. Everything was so bright that I couldn't keep my eyes open anymore. I just passed out from the pain. The old nurse came over and picked me up. I spent about twenty days at the hospital. I came down with malaria, too.

When I got back to my unit I received a letter from my brother Steve and he told me he was in Viet Nam. In the second letter he told me he was in Camp Halloway, which was about five miles from our base camp. When I got back to our base camp, I went over to see him. It was a trip seeing my *carnal* over there. Johnny Guzman from Corcoran was there with him. The day that I got to Nam they passed a regulation that two brothers couldn't be there at the same time. My *carnal* told me it would be better if I would get out of Nam because I was in the infantry and he was in rations breakdown

21

which was a softer job. At this time I was still all pumped and full of shit from basic and AIT. I was still trying to pull the macho bullshit, and I argued that I should stay because I had been there longer. We finally agreed that I should request a leave because my chances were higher of being killed or wounded than his were. The army dragged their feet and ended up taking four months to have me shipped out of Nam.

All of this time I had been lying to my mom. I had told her that I was a truck driver. I changed the story when I got wounded and had to change my address. I told her that I was helping construct a new hospital. I don't think she really believed that, but I think she wanted to believe it. I'm glad they didn't send a telegram home when I got wounded because I don't think she could have taken it. She didn't find out I was wounded until I got home and she saw me without my shirt on when I was combing my hair in the bathroom.

I got to see my brother about four times when I was over there. On January the 6th, 1967, I was asleep when someone woke me up and told me that we were getting mortared. We were up on a mountain, and my brother's camp was about five miles below from us and we could see that they were getting hit harder than we were. The next morning the first thing I did was jump on a truck that was going to town, and from there I got another ride to Camp Halloway. Man! When I got there, there were trucks and buildings all blown up and burned. I finally found my *carnal*. He was all right. He had Johnny Guzman were still kind of scared. These guys were too much because they showed me some little parachutes that they had gotten from the illuminating sky flares. When they were getting hit, they were out in the open running to catch the parachutes for souvenirs. I told them that they were crazy and stupid. Then, they told me that they didn't have any bunkers. They didn't know how to build a bunker, and I showed them how to build one. It's funny because my brother Steve and I never got along as we were growing up. He had his friends and

I had mine. We really didn't treat each other as *carnales* until we saw each other in Nam. We had our first beer together over there.

I was lucky in the sense that we always ran into little parties like six, seven or eight people. We were always about forty guys and right away the guys would throw party on them. I was always in the situation that when we did run into them, they'd run into the squad in front of us. By the time my squad got there, everything was over with. But I still wanted to feel what it was like shooting somebody.

Every time I'd walk the point, my *camarada,* Albert Ortiz, would walk behind me. He told me that if I got into trouble, I should just drop and he would take care of it. He helped me out a lot, he taught me the ropes. Albert was a little *pachuquillo* from Rockhard, Texas. He told me that he got into the army because he got into so much trouble that the cops finally gave him a choice of either joining the army or going to jail.

It was the 24th of December when we were supposed to go in and see the Bob Hope show. Before we could leave, we had to find and clear a landing zone for the choppers so they could pick us up. They gave us the coordinates for one and we found it real quick. But before we could use it we had to secure it. We could see from a distance that there were two hootches on the side of a mountain. We got up to the hootches and checked them out.

By this time I was a squad leader. When we got to the first hootch we knocked down the door. All that was in there was a little bit of rice on the floor and a hammock. We turned around and went into the second hootch. There wasn't anything in there either. At this time, there were only about twenty-five of us because they had gotten a lot of our guys and put them in other platoons that had gotten wiped out. About the time we knocked the second door down, this new guy tapped me on the shoulder and told me that there was a gook in the other hootch. When he said that, I felt all the blood go to my feet. I turned around to the other hootch, which was only about four feet away. The hootch that was supposed to be empty, wasn't. There was a North Vietnamese soldier asleep in the hammock. He had been asleep, so it looked empty. When I turned around into the hootch, he and I looked eye to eye at about three feet from each other. I only had an M-79 grenade launcher so I couldn't shoot him. He looked down and I looked to where he was looking at. There were two grenades on the floor and he reached for them. About that time everybody opens up on the North Vietnamese.

I hit the floor because I couldn't shoot at him. It was too close. They must've shot that guy about two hundred times. Every inch of that hootch was covered with bullets. When the shooting stopped, the lieutenant, who had only been in country for about a month, went in and shot him one more time in the head. One of my *camaradas* picked the gook up, and when he did, I could see one side of his head with the brains hanging out. I can still see that brain, it was gray in color. I could hear his brains sizzling because of all the bullets that hit him. My *camarada* picked him up from the butt and the collar, and I knew exactly what he was going to do, *vatos locos,* you know. He got that guy and he threw him at me. I jumped back and the gook landed about two feet in front of my feet. His brains just went all over my boots. Everybody just busted out laughing. They thought it was the funniest thing in the world.

When we finished laughing, someone suggested that we eat lunch. We started eating, and the platoon leader looked around and said, "Isn't anyone going to bury him or something?" Here you have this guy with his brains sizzling, and by this time, the ants had come around and began to eat on the guy. We began to laugh again. When I was laughing, I was thinking to myself, why in the hell am I laughing, this isn't funny. That's when I started realizing that I wasn't the same person that I was a year ago back in Corcoran. I realized that something had changed in me. I don't think it was for the better, it was for the worse! I hadn't been raised up that way, to be out killing. To find humor in death is when I started realizing I was living like an animal. And pretty soon, you started acting like one.

The platoon leader called up headquarters and informed them of our situation. That North Vietnamese we killed was suffering from malaria and was asleep when we checked out the hootch. He was incapacitated. The reason that North Vietnamese was shot so excessively was that we were full of hate and anger. They had told us that if we made contact we had to stay out in the field. It was the guy's fault that we had to stay out, so everybody threw party on him.

The next day we go back to camp, and I'm still all gung ho about seeing Bob Hope. As soon as I walked into the hootch, one guy told me that I had missed a good show.

After a couple of days, we went back to the field and into Cambodia. I had seen a chopper get knocked down in Cambodia. We were half way up the side of a mountain and the chopper was level to us when it got hit. A rocket hit it and that thing just started burning up and fell. It took us about forty-five minutes to get to the chopper. By that time it was burned up and so was the crew. One guy apparently decided to jump out rather than burn to death. When he hit the treeline, he broke into pieces. We found one of his boots with his foot in it. He must of been a black guy because the skin was black.

When we were putting the remains into green body bags, I began to think. If we get hit and I get burned up, there is no way that my remains are going to get back to my parents. That really bothered me a lot. Something that also bothered me was when I saw people after they had been shot, especially our own, the ants would get there quickly and would begin to eat out the eyes. I remember seeing *vatos* with the mud going in their mouths. I used to think that if I got shot, I didn't want to lie out in the mud and have the ants eating on me.

Soldados

Pulling Listening Post s (LP s) at night was by far the worst experience to go through. Every other night we pulled an LP. For an LP, three guys would go out about three hundred meters from the perimeter and listen for enemy movement. One evening right before nightfall, my team went out on one. We went out about three hundred meters until we came to a fork in the trail. We set up about thirty meters in front of the fork. I thought this would be the perfect place for an LP. It must've been about two in the morning when I started hearing all kinds of stuff. I woke up the other two guys and I told them that somebody was coming at us. I radioed in to the platoon leader and told him we had movement. The platoon leader was green, and instead of telling us to go on in, he told us to wait and see what was happening. Maybe my mind was playing tricks on me, but it sounded like about thirty of them.

By this time they were almost on us. When they came near to the fork, I heard their leader give a command and they halted. It was too late to run back. Then I heard another command and they moved out on line. I thought this guy was going to pull a sweep on us. But instead he called another command and they got back on the trail and went on the trail to the right. I called in and told them we were coming back in. I didn't ask or anything. We just ran as fast as we could. *Hijo de su!* My heart was pounding real hard!

Two days later when we had to go on LP again, I told those in the foxholes to the left and right of us that we were only going about thirty meters ahead. From that day on I didn't go further than thirty meters out.

When I first started fighting the war, I really believed we had a just cause, fighting communism and all of this bullshit they tell you. But after being there awhile, everything changed for me. My main objective was to make it out of there alive. I didn't give a shit who won the war anymore. My whole world had just turned around because I could see a lot of shit that wasn't right. For example, when we went back to base camp,

I'd see all the South Vietnamese soldiers in starch fatigues and waxed–down trucks. there were several times that South Vietnamese units went with us, and they were sorry soldiers. Once the shooting started, the only way we could keep them with us was to literally threaten to shoot them in the back if they ran—and we would have.

Another thing that made me think that way was that people in the United States didn't care about us individually. I finally realized that we were being used. I read a couple of articles in the Stars and Stripes Newspaper that so many congressman had gone to Viet Nam and gotten a firsthand idea of what was going on, and that everything was under control. Hey! I never saw no congressman out in the field. They probably went to Saigon and partied at a couple of nightclubs and came back to the States.

When I was going to college about a year after I got out of the army, I began to listen to what people were saying against the war. It started to dawn on me that I had indeed been used and I hadn't really known what I was doing. I felt angry because I had let that happen to me, and that I had gone along with it.

At the same time I didn't have much of a choice. If I had refused to get drafted, what was I going to do? It would have been just as hard to refuse the draft as it was to go into the army. Where was I going to go? I had nowhere to go. That would have been real hard on my *jefitos*. If people like Jane Fonda had come earlier, there would have been less guys killed in Nam. I go along with what she did.

We were brainwashed into thinking that we had a noble cause, which I don't think we had. The Pentagon under-estimated the North Vietnamese capacity, determinism and their willingness to sacrifice. I had a hell of a lot of respect for them because they knew what they were doing. They were tougher than we were because they didn't get their sundries packed. They didn't get regular mail. They didn't have choppers flying them around. They didn't get to go on R&R.

27

Somebody underestimated them. There are some people who believe that the United States lost the war because the right strategy and tactics were not used. I don't believe that one bit. Anyone who says that was probably never in Nam. And if they were, they weren't in the type of situation to see that it was impossible to do. The only alternative was to use nuclear weapons, and that's no alternative at all.

I had a couple of friends, Jimmy Smith and Burgess, who went over there together so we thought we were all going home together. We agreed that when we got to California, my sister from Watsonville was going to pick us up and take us to her place for a Mexican dinner because Jimmy Smith had never eaten Mexican food. I don't know what ever happened to Burgess, but Jimmy was killed about a month after I left. He got his head chopped off by a helicopter blade. There were a lot of other guys I knew that got killed, and I don't think it was worth it. His wife had a baby while he was in Nam, and Jimmy never got to see that boy.

The day I was leaving Nam, I asked this guy I knew, Danny Rhodes from Lemoore CA, if he wanted me to go see his people and tell them that I was with him and that he was okay. He asked me to go and see his grandfather and grandmother to tell them he was okay. When I got home on leave, Frank Molano, my friend from basic, was home on leave from Panama. One day I asked him if he remembered Danny from basic training and if he wanted to take a drive to Lemoore to see Danny's grandparents. Frank asked me, "Didn't you read the paper? Danny got killed last week." The funeral was the next day, so Frank and I went to the funeral. I remember seeing the grandparents at the funeral, his parents were there, too, but he was raised by his grandparents. I regret that I didn't go up and tell them that I knew Danny in Nam. I didn't know what to say.

When I finally got home from Nam and to my own bed, I slept for something like eighteen hours. My mom finally woke me up because she got scared. When I got home, I was expecting something to blow up any minute. Noises like fire-crackers would make me nervous. Sometimes something would remind me of something that happened in Viet Nam and I would tell my wife and son about it. Even though they've heard it before, they still listen to me. They've been real supportive.

THE CAPTAIN

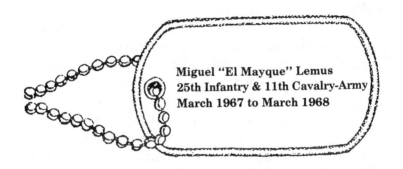

Miguel "El Mayque" Lemus
25th Infantry & 11th Cavalry-Army
March 1967 to March 1968

I was drafted in November, 1967. This was cotton picking season in Corcoran. But, by this time I had moved to San Jose because I couldn't make a living in Corcoran, so I dropped out of high school to help support my family. I am the seventh of eleven kids in my family. In the winter there wasn't any work in Corcoran, but I found work in *Sanjo* as a garbageman, I've been doing it for 23 years. After I started working I went back to school to get my diploma. I was 24 years old when I was drafted. They had been trying to draft me since I was 18 years old. In the end, they decided to take me, but there was no way I was going to volunteer.

For basic training I was sent to Fort Lewis, Washington. It was snowing *de a madre* when I got there. It was always wet. Everything, all of the training was way different from Viet Nam. Fifty per cent of the training wasn't necessary. Viet Nam was a different way of fighting—the way the jungle itself is different. Discipline is what you got out of the Fort Lewis training. It was not like being out in the boonies. Being out in the boonies is something else, when all you want is to make it to the next day. I learned to live day by day. I never thought I would make it back.

I had a thirty day leave before going to Nam. I spent half the time in San Jose and half the time in Corcoran with my mother. She was not happy about it. But she said, "We can't do nothing about it, either you go to Viet Nam or go to jail." She just gave me my blessings and said, "Do the best you can and pray to God you'll be back."

At that time, I said to myself, "Well, in hell I was trained, I guess, in hell I will be." But it didn't turn out that way. I'm here and I guess God himself heard me and decided to keep me alive. But the experience I went through was something else.

Our whole company was taken together. We flew out of Oakland and 19 hours later we were in action. As soon as we landed in Cam Rahn Bay we were bombarded with rockets. All we had to do was find a hole because we didn't have no weapons. This was in March of 1968.

I was with a platoon of Chicanos at the 90th replacement. I was first assigned to the Wolfhounds of the 25th Infantry. Cu Chi was our base and we would go out from there on missions. From there, I went to the 11th Cavalry stationed in Saigon. From there, they put me in the Big Red One—The Iron Triangle—*estaba cabron alli el pedo.* I couldn't believe what happened there. I felt lucky to get out of there alive. From there I went to the 12th Aviation.

They just kept transferring me because I was all forces. I was training guys to use the radio. How to communicate with planes, choppers and artillery, it was my job to keep their asses alive.

The 25th Infantry Wolfhounds was where I saw the most action because we were face to face with the enemy - Viet Cong and some Red Chinese. We were ambushed more than once. Once a battalion of gooks attacked our company. We were hit pretty hard because the gooks were already set up. In the jungle you couldn't see two feet in front of you. Pretty bad. Guys were falling left and right. Some of the guys were being picked off the ground. A lot of them got their heads blown-off, twenty to thirty per cent of the company got wiped out.

They held us there until the 11th Cav and LURP's came in to help us out because we were surrounded. If it wasn't for them . . . it's something that happened so quick. Put it this way, we sucked air through our asses. I did. We were that scared. I was scared, I'm not ashamed to say that, but I fought back. It was quite an experience. Especially for a radioman. The closest a bullet got to me was knocking my radio off my back, that's how close Charlie got to me.

I actually met an enemy soldier face to face! And I respect that son-of-a-bitch. I met him where he could have shot me or I could have shot him. But I guess we both had the same human feeling—that we respected one another. He went his way and I went mine. To explain that I have no words.

Sure, to kill them was my main objective and I had to get them before they got me. But, I don't know . . . I really didn't want to be over there. I felt it wasn't my war. Those people had been fighting for so long and we sure didn't accomplish anything. That's what I had on my mind before even going over. I found out that many soldiers didn't think much about why we were there. In Cu Chi, there were a lot of eighteen and nineteen year old kids and they deserve credit because they were men over there, but nonetheless I found many of them didn't know what was going on over there. They were very scared but I don't blame them. 'Cause training is one thing and being in action is another. 'Cause right there, they sure ain't playing around.

When I got to Viet Nam they made a platoon of all the Chicanos there—all grunts. *Orale, aqui estabamos hablando espanol y la chingada: Habia tres Indios y tres* Chicano radio operators. We worked good because in action I'd use the

Indians to call in their language and sometimes I'd use the Mexicans to call artillery in Spanish. Many times it worked well.

Most of the platoon was from Arizona, New Mexico, Texas and California. I met a lot of *raza* overseas. We got along well. In my company we had to protect each other 'cause no one was going to protect us. As for the races bit, we had to learn to get along because in time of action there was no color. In action everybody works together as a team. That's what got us back. In the rear that's a different story.

In a way, it hurts to think of all of the stuff that I saw over there. I remember one guy died on me as I was carrying him on my back. There were guys that were real happy when they got wounded and were going to be sent home. But, in a way it hurts, because here you have to give up part of your body just to go home. It's something else, but being in hell, I guess you will do anything to get out. It's being there and not knowing if you're going to make it to tomorrow—if you're going to see the sun again. I think being religious helped me. At times I prayed to God, "Keep me alive and bring me back."

El Chicano showed a little bit more anger, more frustration—we thought—what the hell, we're there, and we might as well do it right. We didn't show more braveness on the job or willingness to lose our lives. The Chicano did what he was ordered to do—he didn't hesitate—he would charge.

We'd get like Indians in our all Chicano platoon. We were the wildest bunch. We would bullshit each other until someone would get mad, and sometimes we'd get into a fight. The hell with it, so we'd get pissed and fight. Drinking and *cabula, la raza* - a way of taking out anger and frustrations. And the next day we'd be friends. There were brothers in law, *compadres* and *cabula*, that's what kept the *raza* going.

The *negros* had their thing, but mainly every group in the rear stayed with their own group—*raza* to the *raza*—*mayate* to the *mayate*—*gabacho* to the *gabacho*.

The Puerto Ricans were a lot like the *raza*, in action they all did their job. They were pretty good guys. In the rear they would turn into *indios* and throw *chingazos* like the Chicanos. Everybody was a big family. It was togetherness.

There was everthing—alcohol, weed and cocaine. One time there were ninety of us smoking weed, and over there the weed has a powerful effect. We were getting all crazy and celebrating our return from a mission—well, it was party time. After every goddamned mission we'd party with marijuana and cocaine we got from the gooks, and Uncle Sam gave us the booze. We were crazier than hell, crazy fucking Indians armed with M-16's and drunk. There wasn't any killing of each other than except this one time we came back from a hard mission, it was getting dark and this officer tried to be a hero - bust ninety guys. We were along the trenches and *prata* asshole, they shot him. They threw him over a trench and shot him with a machine gun. No one said anything. Someone called on the radio and told them the captain had been shot by the gooks. Hey, what can I say? It was dark. Who saw it? Nobody saw it? All I saw was the captain. They threw him over and shot him. The gooks got him, I guess.

There was a lot of marijuana being sent to the States during this time. They'd use things like tape recorders to smuggle the weed. It was easy to send weapons like AK-47's. A lot of people made quite a bit of money that way. For me it wasn't worth it, I just wanted to get home in one piece.

I often ask myself, "What did the war prove? Nothing! Was it worth it? No!" I went and saw people get killed and slaughtered for nothing. You can prove you're a man without having to see men get slaughtered. I seen choppers get blown out of the air. Once a whole platoon of infantry was wiped out by gook rockets. Many of them were listed missing in action because there was nothing left of them. What do you tell the parents?

I consider myself very lucky because I came back without a wound. Most of the grunts came back with at least one wound. Maybe not a big one but some sort of mark. And what did that prove? Nothing!

I still hate the gooks. My company never killed women and children, only suspected civilian male gooks. But, there were villages wiped out by artillery or airstrikes. We'd find the gooks in hootches and shoot them. You can lose your cool real easy.

From the infantry I was sent to the cavalry and from there to the 12th Aviation. From there I knew I was going to make it home. It's quite an experience flying around in a helicopter. When you are being shot at from the ground you have no-where to go. Your ass sucks up air, you're scared. You make the sign of the cross and pray to God. But once that's over you get to go back to the barracks and grab a beer *y a toda madre.*

It's different from being in the infantry. In the infantry you stayed with the leeches, bugs and the rain. Being in a tank is like being in a coffin. But that was better than being a tunnel rat. They gave me a 45 pistol with seven bullets—six for the enemy and one for yourself.

I volunteered for these missions because of the hatred I had for the Vietnamese. The hatred started when I seen my sergeant get wiped out right in front of me. I had to pick up the pieces of what was left of the guy. From then it was hatred. I still have it. I see Vietnamese now, but I wouldn't turn around to give them a hand. I ain't going to mess with them unless they mess with me, then they are going to find out who in the hell I am. I'll cut their throats.

I still ask myself why I didn't get killed. What I feel inside of me is bitterness. I hated the South Vietnamese even if they were on our side. I trusted them as far as I could spit and that's up to date. I used those Kit Carson Scouts as pointmen. And if we were going to get ambushed they were going to get it first. I used them like hounds. When some of them got killed it was like who's next. That was it. I had no feelings for those people and I still don't.

I remember soldiers suffering and grabbing me and

saying their last words to me. It hurts. It gives you hatred and you just want to destroy. It gives you a feeling that I can't really express, but it's there. It's a burden that will always be a burden. It's something I have to learn to live with.

Saigon was something else. I went to Saigon on an assignment once. There were to many gooks, so it wasn't really party time. I felt better out in the bush. *Rucas* were three dollars. "Boom, boom baby son three dalla," they would say. They were everywhere, even in the boonies you would meet them. A lot of men made mistakes with the women in the boonies *por que* a lot of them were lured into traps. I seen it. We'd catch those that pulled those tricks and kick their asses. After that we would shoot them in the head and then put our calling card on them. There were many of these *rucas*—quite a few Viet Cong. A lot of them would say they were civilians. Yeah, during the day they might dress civilians, but at night they were Viet Cong. That's one reason I never did trust them.

I was still in action when my time to *DEROS* came up. They picked me out of the boonies, put me on a plane and sent me home. In two days they took me from the boonies to Oakland. I had all of my equipment from Viet Nam. I took a shower in Oakland. I paid a taxi fifty dollars to take me to *Sanjo.*

When I got home, first thing I did was eat tortillas, frijoles and enchiladas—Mexican dinner *de a madre.* All of my family came to see me—I was home. It was something else.

I had *mas coraje que la chingada* when I first came home. I did. Any color of people would piss me off—*mayates, gringos,* anybody. But, as the years went by, I learned to accept. I was taught in the service to survive and if someone wants to mess around with me—O.K. Let's mess around. I was like a young rooster—ready *para tirar chingazos*—no matter what. *Iba a la bara—me ponia pedo—y a tirar chingazos.* But later I found out it wasn't worth it.

I went from a Viet Nam jungle to an American jungle.

Soldados

Except in Viet Nam there wasn't anybody giving you shit orders. *Pinche* M-16 on my side—*orale cabron*—here's your captain - no one was going to mess with me. But here you had people giving you a bullshit order—it doesn't matter who it is—*gabacho, negro*—*orale cabron* here is what you can do with your goddamned order, you Black motherfucker or you white bastard. I don't have to take your goddamned shit. That's the type of attitude I got from Nam.

When I was living at my sister's house, I would still get up in the night—still thinking I was fighting—dreaming that I was still yelling for my men. I still get flashbacks as if I was still in action and in Viet Nam. I see persons I knew and relive when they got shot. I still think back of men dying and asking for the last rites. Mostly *raza*, Catholic religious guys would ask me for the blessing because there weren't any priests out there during the battles.

But it has slacked off now. It's not that I've forgotten but I did have problems for quite awhile—drinking and drugs too. That's why I quit drinking—*me pongo muy indio*.

I learned that I can shoot a person at 3 hundred meters right between the eyes. As long as he is the enemy, I'll wipe him out. I learned a lot in the service but I never did care for it. I just wanted to do my time. I thought I was never coming back. Right now, I have so much hatred toward the Vietnamese that I could go up to them, cut their throats and I wouldn't feel no pity. I have to try and recuperate from all of that.

It's hard to be the same person that you were before you left for the war. Everything changes. Once I was a crazy guy but not anymore. I guess I grew up. But, I don't regret anything. It's an experience I'm beginning to understand - I'm just scratching the surface. I've gone through the worst - what can be worse? I now know how to deal with my stress - how to fight it. Now I've settled down - as long as I am left alone.

I do not recommend any type of war for anyone unless it is declared on us. To me fighting for your rights is justified. But, to go into something that's not our concern is wrong.

Miguel Lemus

Trying to fight somebody in their own land is like trying to fight somebody in their own backyard. You can't mess around with people like that—you end up losing. I think that's what's going on between the United States and Nicaragua. To go to something that's not our concern, I don't see it. Because war is not a good thing, it's a lot of hatred and people getting hurt. And after the war, there is no way to erase the pain and suffering.

WAITING FOR BROTHER

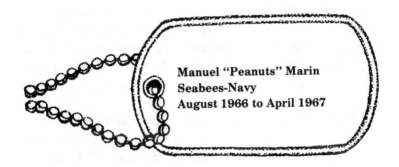

Manuel "Peanuts" Marin
Seabees-Navy
August 1966 to April 1967

T he reason I joined the navy was very simple, I was naive. I saw Pete Garcia with his navy uniform on. I thought he looked sharp. I wanted to wear one. When I was being processed in San Diego, they asked me why I joined the navy. I told them that I had gotten mad at my girlfriend. I'm not sure why I said that. It was partially true, but I guess I wanted to have a manly excuse. I didn't think of myself as a person who planned for the future. I couldn't actually come out and say that once I got out of high school, I planned to be a communications technician for four years. Then I planned to get out and go to college. That was not on my mind, so I had to come out with something and that was the best answer at the time.

One of the reasons that went through my mind for joining the service was that I was once an illegal alien. I was brought over from Mexico at the age of one and being a permanent resident, I felt that it was a good trade for being allowed to live here (U.S.) and go to school. By serving this country, I felt it was a way of paying off. It still goes, regardless of what has happened in between, whether I'd disagree with the politics of being in the service or not. I'm still sincere about this.

When I was about to finish boot camp, they told me that the school for which I had signed up, storekeeper school, was full. So, they told me there were a few other things I could do. I could go on sea duty and eventually I could apply for a school, or I could choose another school that was open. I wanted to go to storekeeper's school because my friend was going. I'm an impatient person. There was no way I was going on a ship and hoped that eventually I was going to get into school. I wanted to get my training then. So, I signed up for electricans' mate school. I didn't know the slightest thing about being an electrician.

I went to electrician school, and I couldn't handle it. I could do the manual part, but I couldn't handle the theory stuff. Some real nice people tried to help me pass the test, but I couldn't do it. That's when the guy in charge called me in and told me I wasn't doing very well on my test. He asked me if I wanted a couple of weeks to see if I could straighten out. I could see that I wasn't getting anywhere. All I was doing was butting my head against the wall. So, I told him to send me out. In my mind, it was almost as if my term of service was going to end quickly by getting rid of this and getting rid of that.

From there I was sent to Coronado, California and there they put me in the worst job possible, which was doing mess hall work. I was there for three months. It was hard work because we'd get up at four in the morning and work until seven or eight at night. After those three months, I was sent to a maintenance unit. That was a lot better because it was an eight to five job. That's when I got into the Seabees.

Most of the sailors that were in maintenance were Seabees and that's how I ended up in Viet Nam. One day we were in the cafeteria drinking coffee. When the chief came in and caught us when we weren't supposed to be there, and we all ran. That's when this one white guy had orders to go to Viet Nam, and he didn't want to go because he was married. That guy was literally crying when he found out. I thought I was on the chief's hit list, so I thought that it was my out if I took that guy's place to go to Viet Nam. I told him to go and tell the chief that I would take his orders.

He ran into the chief's office. When he came back out he told me the chief said he didn't care what we did. Within a day or so, I was getting all kinds of shots and getting ready to go.

One of the reasons I volunteered for Viet Nam, besides trying to get out of trouble, was my impatience. Doing mess hall duty was something I sure as hell didn't want to do for four years. Working in the maintenance crew was not something I wanted do all the time either. I wanted to keep moving. By this time the war was gearing up and we'd hear all kinds of reports. So, that's where I wanted to be, where the war was. I didn't want to be washing dishes and other dumb stuff.

Before we were sent to Viet Nam we were sent to Camp Pendleton for three weeks of training. During the training the Marine trainers were, of course, anti-enemy, but they were also anti-Vietnamese. They would tell us that if we got into a certain type of situation, we shouldn't second guess. To wipe people out because if we didn't we could get killed. I didn't have any experience in those matters, but this Filipino guy named Dan didn't agree with that. He told me that the Japanese did the same thing during World War II, and they killed a lot of children and families. I listened to him and my sentiments were with him because I could relate to the different information from what the trainers were telling us.

Before we left for Viet Nam, the first group of Seabees who had gone to Viet Nam had just gotten back. They were some of the first ones to experience combat, resulting in the deaths of Restituto Adenir and Donald Haskins. When we would talk to them, they gave us the run down on how they saw things over there. They would call the Vietnamese gooks. They told us of how some of the Vietnamese got mad when one of the guys had run over one of their kids and crushed his head. When they told us that, "The gooks were all mad," I could tell right away that there was some kind of insensitivity. These guys knew that they were going to go back because the tours for Seabees in Viet Nam were nine months long, but we had to do two tours.

No matter what the Seabees would tell me, I just took it in stride. I was thinking, "Yea, I'm tough. I want to go over there and the sooner the better. Let's go over there and see what's happening." I had no idea what the war was about. I was just thinking that I was on one side and the enemy was on the other and let's duke it out and let's see what we can do. I was thinking I was going to be the hero . . . I was going to be a big shot. Of course, everything turned out completely different from what I thought it was going to be. That was because of fate and the type of unit I was in. We were a construction battalion and not an infantry unit. That made a lot of difference, but that didn't mean, being the type of war that it was, that we were immune to getting blown up in our truck or little hootch. The fact was that I was just real lucky.

One of the first things we did when we got to Red Beach, right outside of Da Nang, was fill sandbags. We filled sandbags, my God, it seemed like for two or three weeks. I hated that. I thought it was stupid because we had all kinds of training and here we were filling sandbags. Our batallion commander would come by and tell us we were doing a good job and that we had to get everything squared away soon. He was right. But being naive, you don't think about being prepared. I remember the commander making a comment about expecting an attack from the north. As soon as he walked away, I thought he was just harassing us into filling the son-of-a-bitching bags. As I read the history now, the attack did come from the north. It came about two or three hundred yards from where our camp was. This happened when Viet Nam fell to the north, but it did come. He was right in some sense, but for us who were filling sandbags, it was a completely different view. The batallion commander was responsible for a thousand men and we were just thinking about our individual selves.

As we were filling sandbags, we were also building up our perimeter and camp. Our next project was to provide services for the Air Force and Marines. We built mess halls, hootches and bases. Our daily routine was very predictable. We'd wake up at a certain time, go to work at seven, eat at the same times and in the evenings do basically the same things. This wasn't a good practice because the enemy knew exactly what to expect from us.

I never felt better than the village people and I didn't hate them. I may have sensed that I was better off than they were. But to call them names and not respect them is one thing I never did. There were some incidents that happened in which I felt sorry for the Vietnamese. I used to work with some Vietnamese once in a while. They used to do hard labor. With the Vietnamese that I got to know well, there was like a taking to each other. There was an attempt to communicate with each other. I remember this one guy walking up to me and pointing to my arm and then to his arm, indicating that we were the same color. I was the only Mexican on that project and he could relate to my physical characteristics. I felt pretty good about that. Now, in terms of what I felt about the enemy, I didn't have any reservations about duking it out with them. If I was attacked, there wasn't time to say, "Hey, you're nice people."

I was bored working in our base camp. My squad took off and they went to work in a special forces camp. They took about twelve people and I wasn't chosen to go. About a week after they left, the company commander went to review the job. We were drinking beer when he came back and told us that he needed more men over there. I remember telling him that I would really appreciate it if he would send me out there. He said, "If you see what's out there, you won't appreciate me sending you over there. The whole place is surrounded by VC." I didn't care, I wanted to get the hell out of there. He told me that I would be one of the two men that he was going to send. I think he chose me because he knew I was a hard worker and probably because this guy named Mule recommended me. I was tickled to death because I was chosen.

The night before I was to leave, I had a dream where I envisioned the place I was going to be in. My dream was not too far from what the place was like, except that it was on a much larger scale. I remember real vividly that there was like a barbed wire fence around our camp and it was surrounded by trees.

Getting to Houng Duc was an experience. We went on one of those caribou airplanes. When the plane landed on the dirt runway, there wasn't anybody to meet us. I got scared as I got off the plane because there were a lot of Vietnamese all around us. I panicked and put a clip in my rifle. Pretty soon here comes this jeep and as it turned out, it was a Chinese guy that didn't speak any English. I panicked even more because I thought that maybe it was a set up. It turned out okay. He was a Chinese mercenary working for the South Vietnamese.

We worked there with the Green Berets for three months. What we basically did was build a huge ammunition and communication bunker. There were about twenty Seabees, twelve Green Berets and forty Vietnamese. If you have seen the movie, *The Green Berets,* that's exactly what that base was like. Houng Duc was an observation post and it was about twelve miles from the Laotian border. A couple of years before the whole war ended, the enemy sent swarms of troops and took over the camp. We were lucky we weren't overrun because we were really outnumbered out there. My best project was the one with the Green Berets because at that time, and even now, they carried weight. The Green Berets deserve a lot of credit because they were brave. They were put in situations that were very difficult. If they got out without injuries, it was rare.

Even though we were surrounded by the enemy, we were not overrun because we had too much firepower and support. That's probably why we were only mortared once during the time I was there. On another tough occasion, we were in a fire fight for about three hours. The machine guns were going on all the time. Most of the time I was assigned to shoot flares. We also got some help from Da Nang. They brought Puff the Magic Dragon and he did his thing. In the morning when the whole thing was over, there was smoke all over the valley at the bottom of the hill.

After that project was over, I went back to Da Nang for about a month before I was sent to the Mekong Delta. We were the first Seabee unit to be sent down there. Our project was to build sleeping quarters for the sailors that were working off the PT boats. An army unit from the Ninth Infantry was sent in to protect us. That place was real easy to be attacked because we were surrounded by jungle. Right before we got there, a mortar had landed in the perimeter. For those two weeks that we were there, those one-o-five guns didn't stop all night long. They just kept going and going. It was hard to sleep but the Viet Cong or NVA never bothered us. Later when we left, I read in the Stars and Stripes that they hit that base hard.

The Green Beret place and the Mekong Delta projects were where the enemy had their chances on me, but they didn't capitalize. Fate had a lot to do with what took place and what happened to me. We finished the project in record time. The supervisors were so impressed that they gave us two days in Saigon. We got to party down in Saigon. That was good but it was too fast, and you get in trouble there real quick.

And that was it. After that, we came back to the Camp Adenir, we just (for the next few weeks that were left) did odds and ends. I think I came back to the United States on the twelfth of April, and my brother Julian got to Viet Nam about the same time. I remember he was killed about two weeks after he was there.

We stopped in Japan on the way home and I remember seeing a lot of soldiers there at Yokota. I remember feeling kind of sad. I was hoping that I would see Julian. I knew he was going to Viet Nam because he wrote to me. He was telling me that it was time for me to come home. I think he felt like I did at one time, I guess he was naive in some ways. He was saying that I should be hurrying home because I deserved to hurry home and that it was time for him to go over there and take care of things. He was thinking it was going to be real easy for him, but I think all soldiers in general think that way—at least the more naive ones. The ones who are more mature, the most up to date . . . they sense something and say, "Hey, I'm not going to get into that position."

My family was telling me that at first he was kind of reluctant to go into the army. Someone was telling him that they would send him to Mexico, but he said no because he had to do his part. I heard all kinds of rumors about his first assignment. That's what I heard from a couple of guys from Corcoran that were in the Twenty-Fifth Infantry. The rumor has it that nobody wanted to be the point, so he volunteered to do it but those are rumors, and it's neither here nor there. That's why I would like to get the battle reports of what happened. However, I do know that most of the soldiers who went out on that night ambush were killed because the army sent us a list of the twelve soldiers that were killed. He was killed by a claymore mine.

It devastated my family, but I guess it was my mom who took it the hardest. Men, you know, are kind of more reserved. We suppress our feelings more. They come out when you're alone. I don't think I've ever seen my dad cry for Julian except for maybe once or twice. And even then, I'm not sure if it was regarding the death of Julian. But most of the time he kind of explained things to himself. I guess his view was that it was fate and there was nothing we could do.

As for me, it's very complex because I think of it in terms of the rumors that I heard, I consider the letter that he sent me, I consider that there's still MIAs, I consider the fact that I didn't see him before we buried him or supposedly buried him. Nobody saw him. We had a chance to see him but they recommended that we didn't see him, because he was mutilated. So, every time I see that MIA list, even though this is years and years later, I keep hoping that Julian is alive. There is always some hope, I guess, even though the chances are not there.

One of the things that I advise people not to do, being a wise man now, is that if you're ever in that situation, don't ever do what I did—bury somebody without seeing him, which was a real stupid thing to do. At first you rationalize it. The thing is, you're darned if you do and you're darned if you don't. If you see that the person is really mutilated, that stays on your mind, on the other hand, if you don't see that person, especially being in war and overseas, how do you know he is dead? When I read those reports that there are still MIAs and all of that, I'm still thinking that in the middle of chaos, they grabbed Julian and took him. And somebody else got killed and a mistake was made and Julian didn't return. It is easy to make mistakes like that. But anyway, I'm certain that he is dead, but I guess it is always going to be there—the doubt. That is a difficult situation to be in.

I've had my problems dealing with the Viet Nam War. There are times that I feel that I didn't do enough because I wasn't an infantry person. There was a time that I mortared a village. Somebody fired at one of our airplanes from the village. I was part of a mortar crew when that happened, and I dropped 20 mortars in the tube and another guy dropped about five more. I always knew that I had done that. It took me until a couple of years ago to really begin to deal with it. For a lot of years, I thought that the stress syndrome was a figment of a person's imagination, or that maybe it was people who did real cruel things and they were suffering for it now. I never considered myself one of those persons. I always thought that I could handle it. I don't know what made me feel like this. Was it time or was I just debating the war experience in my mind? Then one day I asked myself, what if I killed women and children? That's one thing I'll never find out.

I understand a little more now and I'm hoping, against the odds, that we will never go to war again. I think it's futile. It is very difficult to understand how 58,000 people died and see that nothing good came of it. I would like to see the U.S. in a defensive position, but that's not the case. We (U.S.) are real contradictory. We'll say human rights are okay over here but not over there. Intervention is okay one place but not another. That kind of a policy is real inconsistent and dangerous in the long run. I'm apprehensive about the outcome in that respect.

ACE OF SPADES

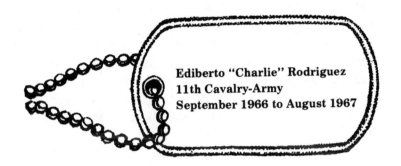

**Ediberto "Charlie" Rodriguez
11th Cavalry-Army
September 1966 to August 1967**

I was working for Gilkey Farms when I was drafted into the army on October 7, 1965. I took basic training at Fort Ord, California. The whole squad I was in were Chicanos from Corcoran. There was Henry Torres, Gopher, Joe-Mama, and Larry Gomez. After basic training, I was the only one sent to Fort Meade, Maryland from my squad. During this time, Fort Meade was a Replacement Depot. They would send people overseas from there.

As soon as I got there, they told us that our unit, the 11th Cavalry, was being built up to be sent to Viet Nam. Because of this, I didn't go through my advanced infantry training. Instead, they had me pulling guard duty and doing KP.

There were protesters at Fort Meade all the time I was there. Every weekend we used to go to Washington, DC, which was only twenty miles from there. We would have a lot of meetings during the week about problems we would have with the protesters. We didn't like the protesters. Quite a few guys used to get into fights with them. A lot of times the soldiers would go into DC with their uniforms on and some people would hassle them, and the soldiers would fight them. Sometimes the soldiers didn't even have to be hassled in order to start a fight, especially if they had been drinking. They used to tell us in company meetings, "If you're going to get into a fight, get into a good fight and do it right, because you're going to jail—so you might as well fight to win."

That's one of the things that was unique about the 11th Cav. If you went out downtown or the village to party, and someone was getting into a fight with someone from another unit, everybody would stick together and fight. One time in Bien Hoa, Viet Nam, the 11th Cav got into a fight with the 173rd Airborne and the Air Force. No one got killed, but it was a pretty mean fight. The 11th threw those guys out of their own club. I think we really stuck together as a unit because we all started together.

A couple of months had passed by when one day I looked out the window and there were all kinds of recruits coming down the street. Then they told us that we were going to have a two-week leave before we moved out. So I took my two-week leave and then went back to Maryland. A little later, we moved out. We took everything we had. The only things we left were the bunks and mattresses. When we got on the plane, we had our steel pots and rifles with us. From Maryland they flew us to Travis Air Force Base, California. A bus took us to Oakland where we boarded the ship which took us to Viet Nam.

The trip took about three weeks. We'd get up at four in the morning to do two hours of physical training, then we would have classes through out the day. There were about 1,500 of us, so we didn't have to pull too many details. Since we went over as a unit, we were psyched-out. Everything was Viet Nam. Once we got there, we had to wait for our equipment to arrive. This helped us get accustomed to the idea of being in Viet Nam. Before our equipment arrived, we were sent on a mission because too many of the guys were just getting drunk and messing up.

Our unit was one of the first units to get to Long Binh. We had sent an advanced party about thirty days before we got there to clear the area. After the main body arrived, we secured a larger area and provided support for the 199th Light Infantry Brigade. In fact, we escorted them to Long Binh. The 11th Cav was unique because we didn't need support. We had everything we needed. We had tanks, armored personnel carriers, howitzers, helicopters and some mechanized infantry. It got pretty rough at times riding those tracks. Every time we had straight leg infantry work with us, we'd have a couple of them fall off the tracks. It would get real hot inside those tracks, something like 140 to 150 degrees. It would get so hot that the grease in the grease guns would run out.

In Long Binh we'd get sniper fire everyday and mortar fire every so often. The first mission we went out on, when all of our equipment arrived, we had some small arms and mortar fire. When we were coming back from that mission, one of our platoons got ambushed. We had so much fire power that we had a body count of about 130 to 140 dead VC. It was a VC battalion that ambushed our platoon. The platoon had about twelve people killed. That's not bad considering the damage they did to the Viet Cong.

They got hit with everything. Some of those tracks were blown up and burned real bad. The first platoon was the one who got hit first. They got hit with recoilles rifles, mortars, RPG's, armour piercing rounds, and stuff like that. The first couple of drivers never knew what hit them. I opened the door to one of the trucks that was being escorted. It had been hit and caught on fire. As I looked in the truck, this one guy said, "Look at those two guys." All I could see was ashes. I didn't bother to take another look.

The 11th Cav was the "it" unit in our area of Viet Nam. We had less casualties and more VC body count than other units. We could move from one point to another in full force faster than other units could. Yeah, other units could get there a little faster. Other units would put them on cargo planes, and then they had to set up and stuff like that. In the process , they would get their asses kicked. I remember one time a company from the 173rd Airborne, which was situated next to the Cambodian border, was overrun. We went over to help them, and the Viet Cong only snipered at us. The Viet Cong wouldn't hit us like they did other units because we had too much fire power. We never had anybody wiped out. I remember one time, however, that we did get hit hard. We got mortar and rocket fire for about two hours. Most of the guys were sleeping in their foxholes when we got hit. We used to dig foxholes to sleep in, but our fighting positions were on the tracks. When we got hit like that, we'd open up with the fifty caliber machine guns. We always set up in an open field. We had so much fire power that we didn't have to hide. Another time we got hit going down Highway 13. On this operation we had our 175 howitzers, the kind that are mounted on tracks. A Viet Cong ran about 30 yards in front of the howitzer. Well, the howitzer fired one of those shotgun rounds at the VC. We never found one piece of him.

The Viet Cong were just like us; they were doing their job. I was over there because I was sent there. I was also doing a job and being patriotic my country.Whether the war was right or wrong was not up to me to decide. I would have probably even volunteered for Viet Nam, but the CO back at Fort Meade told me it was not necessary because we were all probably going to Nam. I wanted to see some action, and I was also tired of pulling guard duty and KP.

The South Vietnamese soldiers were meaner with their own people than we were. Once, this CIA guy and an interrogator from the South Vietnamese Army had this kid about 16 years old, and he was scared. They kept asking him questions and he kept saying that he didn't know. I was standing there watching because I was assigned to guard him. All of a sudden, the South Vietnamese interrogator hits him on the jaw with the butt of his rifle and knocks him down, and the kid starts crying.

The Korean soldiers were even meaner. We were going down the road once and this sniper shot at them (Korean soldiers). One Korean soldier blew a whistle and they went straight into the jungle. The VC were scared of them because the Korean soldiers didn't give a shit. You shoot at them and they went right after you, and they didn't take prisoners either.

By about the seventh month I was there, I had had a lot of close calls. For awhile I was thinking of doing another year in Nam, but only if they would make me a door gunner on a helicopter. I asked the Colonel to assign me, but he wouldn't do it. Then I figured that the odds were against me, so, I didn't volunteer for another year. Four guys out of my section had not been wounded; I was one of those guys.

Only one guy was killed from my section during the whole time I was there. He was kind of prejudiced. He was a *gabacho*, and he didn't like Mexicans. As time went by, he was more accepting of Mexicans. Once, me, him and this Puerto Rican were playing cards and he came up with this shit, "Hey, let's see who's going to die over here." He got so many cards and spread them apart, and whoever picked the ace of spades was going to die: the ace of spades was the death card over there. If nobody got it, nobody was going to die over there. I was the first one to pick a card, then the Puerto Rican, then he picked. He picked the ace of spades. Then he said, "Hey, that's not right, let's pick again." So he spread the cards out again. I picked first, then the Puerto Rican, and then he picked the ace of spades again. "This is not fair," he said. "You guys picked first." He shuffled the cards again. This time he chose first and he picked up the ace of spades. He picked it up three times in a row and he died over there. I don't believe in that shit, but it happened. He was kind of depressed a little bit afterwards. We used to play fucked up games like that all of the time. Some of those bastards were playing Russian Roulette. We used to do things that I would never think of doing now.

About twenty minutes before we started out on the mission that that guy was killed on, I was talking to a guy who owed me twenty dollars. I had lent it to him to go on R&R. He was looking for a track to ride on. "Get on my track," I told him, "you owe me twenty dollars, I want to make sure you make it to pay day. I'll take care of you, I'm a good driver." The guy said, "Naw, I'm going on radio watch in a couple of hours and it's better if I ride in the track in front of you. Naw," he said, "I'll be all right in this track." I said, "Hey, come back, I've got to protect my investment, come back here." He got on the track that was to hit the mine. They sent him back to the States, his ribs were broken by the mine explosion. He mailed me my twenty dollars. He was a *gabacho* from Massachusetts.

Every so often, we would go through Saigon, always at night. Anything that was walking out there, we could shoot. When we went through that town, the vibrations could be heard two or three miles down the road. Long Gao means, "Home of the Dragons." The Vietnamese people named us that because we had huge flame throwers and all kinds of destructive vehicles and equipment. We used to travel a particular part of highway, it was called Thunder Road, because you could hear us coming down the road just like thunder.

We used to make the Stars and Stripes Newspaper all of the time because we never got our asses kicked and we never killed innocent civilians. Once in a while, some innocent people got killed because they were caught in the crossfire. But we never went and killed any civilians or destroyed anything intentionally. The only complaint that I knew of was that we were ruining rubber trees. North of Long Binh there were some beautiful rubber plantations. I once saw the fantastic house of one of the plantation owners. It had an Olympic size swimming pool.

A little ways from the house was a small village with a couple of bars and a whore house. So I said to myself, "I might as well get myself a piece since I'm here." This dumb Chicano from Fresno who had just gotten there, he had been there for a about a month, was there all *escamado.* He was guarding the little road that led to the village. By this time I was talking to him, three or four more tracks arrived. He said, "Hey man, look at those tracks. They've got some mean guns on those tracks." He kept on talking, "You know, we killed a VC the other day and we carved a big red one on his chest, *y la chingada.*" I told him, "We don't even bother to count them anymore, we kill so many of them. It's too much trouble to keep count. Just keep an eye on me with that 60 machine gun. I'm going into the bar."

As I was turning I saw some montagnards with bright orange teeth coming towards me. They got those orange teeth by chewing some sort of nut. They were riding bicycles and they had crossbows. I was unarmed because it was an in-formal rule that we were not allowed to carry weapons into the bars. So then, those guys jumped off their bikes and I thought, *"A la madre,* I've had it, this is it." I was getting ready to push them off their bicycles. They jumped off the bicycles and extended their crossbows towards me. They just wanted to sell them crossbows to me. I didn't buy them. Instead, I went into the bar for a piece of ass and a couple of beers. The girls there were okay, but I like the Cambodian women best because they had big knockers.

I got a thirty-day cut in my tour. I was so busy with my duties that I didn't have time to think about leaving Viet Nam. The last few days I was there, I went to see Louis Lerma from Corcoran, who was stationed at Ben Hoa. Rudy Leon had given me his address. I ran into Rudy Leon at a village bar. As I went into the bar, I saw him standing there. He looked at me and said, "Charlie, is that you?" I said, "Yea, it's me." He was getting ready to go back to his camp. "Let's get drunk one of these days," I invited. *"Orale ese,"* he said. I asked him where he was staying so I could go over. He told me I couldn't. Other units that were attached to us couldn't carry their rifles around. They couldn't do this and they couldn't do that. They had to be in bed at a certain time. In our unit we would get twenty-dollar fines if we didn't carry our rifles and ammunition. They had a lot of regulations, whereas in our unit, as soon as we were done with our duties, we could do things other people were not allowed to.

COMMENTS, NOTES
AND RECOLLECTIONS
OF WILLIE ALVIDREZ

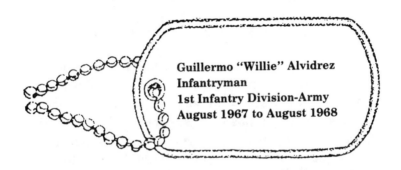

Guillermo "Willie" Alvidrez
Infantryman
1st Infantry Division-Army
August 1967 to August 1968

A t first I was the radioman, then I became the grenadier. Afterwards, I was a rifleman and an assistant machine gunner. I even carried the flame thrower for a while. I went back and forth. All that to get away from being pointman, Because he was usually the first one to get it.

★ ★ ★ ★ ★ ★ ★ ★ ★ ★ ★ ★ ★

I arrived in the Republic of South Viet Nam on August 27, 1967 by way of TWA (The Wrong Airline). We landed at Bien Hoa Air Force Base. There were soldiers at the air field who had completed their tours and we quickly grew envious of them. From Bien Hoa they took us to a transit company in Long Binh. My first assignment was KP. I started the detail around five in the afternoon, and I was supposed to stay until morning because they had guys coming and going twenty-four hours a day. I was tired from the trip, so I skipped out and went to the barracks around 9:00 p.m. Soon after leaving the mess hall, the base was hit by a mortar barrage and by a ground attack on the other side of the perimeter. I used that as an excuse for not returning to KP. We were in bunkers, but I decided to get out because it was too stuffy inside the bunkers. I entered the barracks and found a bed with a mosquito net around it and went to sleep. A Mexican buck sergeant found me and said I had to go back to the bunkers. Later, I snuck out and went to sleep underneath a bed in one of the barracks.

I got hit 27 days prior to coming home. A piece of shrapnel hit me in the left shoulder. It was only a superficial wound. I was lucky. I got scared because all this time I had gone without a scratch. I thought I was invincible. I never received my purple heart; my platoon leader reported it, but the first sergeant never did. He was a drunkard. I really don't care about the award because I have the shrapnel as a souvenir.

At the combat indoctrination school, which took five days, we were given a refresher course of the things we had learned at Fort Jackson, South Carolina. That night we were hit by mortars. All this was during their elections. I don't even recall who was running for president.

My first operation with my unit was road clearing along with the Army Engineers. They cleared the roads with mine detectors while we provided security. Almost every night the

Viet Cong planted mines on the roads in order to knock out Army vehicles. After road clearings in the afternoons, we set up outpost until the evening. At dusk we set up listening post. We didn't spring any ambushes on that operation even though we set three a week. A personal carrier detonated a land mine and a second lieutenant was killed. That was the only casualty on that operation. It lasted 30 days.

When I arrived to my unit about 60 per cent of the troops were either Black, Puerto Rican or Mexican/Chicano. However, it changed during the course of my tour. After a while, we started getting more Anglos who had been college students or who were married. During war or a conflict, the military will lower their mental and physical standards. By doing this, they snare more men. I had scoliosis of the spine when I was inducted, and my condition was aggravated by the hard patrols. The flame thrower alone weighed fifty pounds.

It was about forty days after I had arrived in Viet Nam that we were ambushed in the Iron Triangle. It was a North Vietnamese and Viet Cong stronghold. It was called the Iron Triangle because it formed a triangle on the map. We usually worked war zones A and D and the Michelin rubber plantation. One day our battalion was ambushed about 1000 meters away from our base camp. Our battalion commander took the same route three times in a row. He did this because he did not want to cross the river and go through the swamp. He took the easy way. On the third day we got hit. He got it too. Headquarters company along with A and B and a recon platoon were hit very hard. There were about two hundred and fifty G.I.'s killed in that ambush, with about a dozen survivors. I am not really sure of the exact number of dead. It could have been more. The reason I didn't know is that it was never reported. The newspapers back around October of 1967 only mentioned that some officers had been killed in an ambush.

On the third day of the operation, which was named Operation Shenandoah, my company stayed back to guard our base camp. It was an L-shaped ambush and it lasted for about ten minutes. We were told over the horn that our battalion had suffered heavy losses. When the dozen or so survivors reached our perimeter, they were in a daze and incoherent with shock. "Help us," they said. "We need help out there." They had panicked and thrown away their weapons and gear. The G.I.'s who were still alive after the ambush were shot in the head by the North Vietnamese.

I only saw about five dead North Vietnamese; our guys hadn't managed to fire many rounds. Our artillery buried a lot of the G.I.'s because the artillery was called in that close. The enemy was camouflaged and dug in a few meters from our people. The ambush happened about noon; we policed bodies until about six that evening. Medivac after Medivac landed and took off. The next day we gathered bodies from about 7:30 in the morning until three in the afternoon. We were relieved by the 2nd Battalion/18th Regiment.

The fault for this ambush lay with the battalion commander who didn't follow the rules. We used to have rules dating back to the colonial days of Major Rogers. He had established the rules of never using the same trail twice, walking single file and five meters apart. We were losing whole companies of men in Viet Nam during this time and they didn't report it.

When I was there, everybody was the same—equal. Everybody looked after each other equally. We didn't have many cultural clashes or anything like that. Everybody got along. They were thinking about survival. There was some segregation back in the rear, but no discrimination.

Around June of 1968 one of my best friends, Marvin Scott from Michigan, got shot in the chin. He choked on his own blood. This was about four days after we got ambushed in war zone D. We suffered a lot of casualties that day.

When I got hit, it was by a grenade launcher. We were reconning an ambush site. That is, we would set up ambushes in areas we thought they would try and ambush us. Many times we were so exhausted from the day patrols that we would fall asleep. They worked us like dogs all day long and then we would have to pull guard at night every three hours. Replacements were slow, and we never got more than six at a time. We had to do the work of two or more men.

We started getting extra heavy contact, so I put in for R&R. I had thoughts of going AWOL from there. I went to Kuala Lumpur, Malaysia. It used to be a British commonwealth. The people there are mostly Indian, Chinese and Australian. I had put in for Australia because I wanted to get Away from Orientals. But I couldn't get it because there were too many people who had the same feelings. I had a Chinese wife and Tiger beer for five days. I waited eight months before I put in for R&R.

After B-52 bombers were called in, we would find a few dead bodies in the area, or maybe some arms or legs and stuff like that. They would vanish, it seems, into thin air or underneath the earth. We didn't know very much about their tunnel complexes.

I got busted once for having a good time, too many parties. I went AWOL three times. They gave me a break and gave me special court-martials: seventy dollar fines and a reduction of rank from E-3 to E-2. We were making a lot of contact. That's why they gave me a break. I went AWOL because when we came in from the field we had to pull tower guard. So we rebelled and went to the bars. I was what they called a juicer. That is, I did not smoke marijuana—it was too hot to smoke that stuff. I usually drank French beer, wine, or Japanese whiskey. I didn't see anything wrong with taking a day off after those long patrols. I was a rebel, but I did my job out in the field.

We had a barrack-full of guys waiting for court-martials for refusing to fight. They felt it wasn't worth it. We didn't know the terrain and we were getting ambushed too often. I can't say I blame them, but I completed my whole tour.

One of my uncles was killed in World War II. He was also in the 1st Infantry Division. One of our cousins served in the

82nd Airborne and he was also killed. I have three brothers who were with the 1st Cavalry Division during the Korean Conflict.

I woke up one morning and I couldn't breathe from hyperventilation. Then I started losing weight. I lost forty pounds—I went down to 145. I couldn't breathe properly for two years. I couldn't sleep, I would pace up and down for hours at a time. They gave me tranquilizers at the VA hospital. I suffer from insomnia, fatigue, a lack of concentration, nervousness, hypertension and hypersensitivity to light (photosensitivity). I became ill about a year after I was separated from the service, and to date, I still don't feel up to par. I really don't know what caused my condition. For all I know, it could have been agent orange or that I suffer from delayed stress syndrome. I receive some compensation from the Veterans Administration.

Politically, I didn't even think about it, the war. I just thought about surviving the year or perhaps going to Leavensworth or Long Binh Jail (LBJ). If I hadn't been drafted, I don't think I would have volunteered. I would have volunteered if the U.S. was in danger of being invaded.

I had some resentment toward the South Vietnamese because they didn't want to do their job. The ARVNS refused to help themselves. Either they were tired of the war or were spoiled by the American troops who took over the war. However, we can't blame the ARVNS for everything. We also didn't have to much incentive to fight. The United States said we were fighting for freedom. Yet, we heard all about their government corruption and the protesting in the United States. I guess surviving was the key incentive that kept us going.

I heard they started fighting again, the underground. But how come they didn't help themselves then—back in 1968. They were receiving massive amounts of arms and equipment. But I must admit they were pretty good at riding their motorcycles.

Two platoons ambushed each other. A bible stopped the bullet from hitting one of the soldiers in the chest. He thought it was a bad omen and refused to go on any further. He was court-martialed. A Chicano from LA was also shot in a leg and it had to be amputated.

The guys used to buy marijuana for five dollars a sandbag. A case of beer, a bottle of wine, and a woman were also five dollars.

Can you imagine the mentality of the officers? We even tried ambushes using tanks and APC's. Why, they could hear us setting up the ambush from far way, and then we were not to make any noise afterwards. The leadership was not too good.

Lt. Calley was following orders. He was made a scapegoat because they needed someone to take the blame. My first platoon leader, Lieutenant Bracy, who was a soul brother, was relieved from his duty because of an incident. A spotter plane was shot down and we had to secure it. They told the lieutenant we should break to the right when we got off the helicopter. It should have been to the left. Somebody else made the blunder and he took the blame. I don't think it was because he was Black. A lieutenant has to follow orders, too.

THE GUARDSMAN

Benny L. Molina
National Guard
Watts and Berkeley Riots
1965 and 1968

I was driving truck for Villanueva Trucking out in Sacramento when I was called up by the Guard and told to report to Fresno. The guys who were close to Fresno got there first and they were taken on C-130s to Los Angeles. It took me several hours to get there, so I drove a truck in a convoy to Watts. It took me four days to meet up with my company. We spent a total of three weeks in Watts. I tell my old lady that I was in war, and she doesn't believe me. But it was a combat situation. People were hostile.

I just wonder how many people actually got killed in the riots. I know that it was more than thirty-eight people reported killed. The police and the National Guard killed most of them. We worked along with the police, and sometimes they wouldn't go without us because we had automatic weapons.

All the time that we were there, martial law was in effect. There was a curfew and nobody was supposed to be out in the streets. We could shoot anybody who was not supposed to be out at night. One night, we were helping guard a police station when one of the police sergeants told me that a man was going to come out of this particular house at four in the morning to catch his ride. I told him that I was glad he told me because our guys were ready to shoot anything.

We went out on a lot of night patrols to enforce the curfew. We'd pass by the bars and the owners would fill our helmets with beer, they were glad that we were there to protect their property. We mostly had to worry about snipers and molotov cocktails. One night we went out in a deuce-and-a-half truck when we began to receive sniper fire. That's when a major came along and asked us what we were doing under the truck. As soon as he said that, we were fired upon again. He jumped under the truck real quick. There was a second Lieutenant Heinz in the cab and he got underneath the dashboard. After that, we called him "Air Conditioner" Heinz because he fit under the dashboard just like an air conditioner.

We hardly got any sleep. The only time we got time to sleep was during the day and it was too hot to sleep. Those people who were rioting didn't know what they wanted. Why would they burn the grocery stores down? Then later on they were begging for food.

The cops and us used to carry throw-away-knives. The cops still do. Those were knives we used to carry in case we shot somebody we weren't supposed to. If that happened, the knife is placed by the body to make it seem as if the victim was armed.

We had some Blacks in our unit and I would tell them I was going to put them in front when we were on patrol because they wouldn't be shot. They were black. The Blacks were scared because they were like traitors being in the National Guard and going against the rioters.

I probably would have had the same attitude if the rioters had been Chicano. It's like while I'm working for the Guard and some *camarada* tells me, "Come on, give me a break." I tell them, "If I give you a break that means I have to do the work." That's my way of thinking. In those days if the rioters would have been Chicano, hey, *te chingaste, baboso*. It's either you or me, and I'd rather that it be you.

Compared to Watts, Berkeley was a piece of cake. Those people (rioters) thought we were just fresh from Viet Nam because of our uniforms and all. Everything was hush, hush. They used to tell us not to talk to anybody unless we got permission, and not to talk to the news media. We spent about seventeen days in Berkeley. They were just a bunch of hippies, but martial law was declared there, too.

I never got the CIB (Combat Infantry Badge) but I did get the NRB (Nigger Riot Badge) and HRB (Hippie Riot Badge).

MARINE

Larry "Horse" Holguin
Infantryman-Delta One-Four
Third Marine Division
June 1968 to September 1969

I didn't want to go back to the Marines after my thirty day leave. I already had my orders cut out for Nam and I didn't really want to go. My dad told me to go because he taught us that you never cop out on nothing. If you do something, you do it all at one time: never back off from nothing. I followed his rules because, as far as he had taught me, it never hurt me. I had volunteered on my own, so I had to finish it.

I was scared on the plane trip to Viet Nam because I didn't know what to expect. When I landed, the red clay was the first thing I noticed. That really made me feel far away, different. I remember I lit a cigarette up and it was so humid that I couldn't smoke, I coughed it up. But what I remember the most was when I arrived at Dong Ha. I remember I walked to the tent area where the guys were. I walked in and there were three guys standing around a helmet. One guy had an M-14 in his hand and was breaking the fingers of another guy with the steel plate butt of the rifle. It was strange. I saw the

73

guy a few months later and his fingers didn't heal right. They had to go back and re-break all of his fingers. He did it because he didn't want to go back to the bush. He had been through some bad shit, so it is only normal that he would try that in the long run. I was in Dong Ha for a week of training, when I first seen an American guy dead. He got killed when he stuck his head up from a foxhole and the concussion blew his head off.

When I got to my unit, Delta one-four, all of the Marines were hurting and thirsty. They asked for my water and kept it. I remember two mountains that were flattened out by artillery and all the vegetation knocked out. It was hot and the Marines smelled bad.

By the second week, we hit the shit. I remember I didn't fire a round either. I could see the gooks running around and AK's going off. You could hear the difference between the AK's and the 16's. I remember I was on top of something that was hot, but I didn't feel the heat until afterwards because it started blistering on me. After about 15 or 17 dudes got off the choppers, we made a small perimeter. Then we started going down in what they call "in line". There was a lot of yelling and stuff going on. I don't really remember seeing anything. We stayed there that night. We had a lot of enemy movement that night.

We did a lot of walking. The part about sleeping was the weirdest thing because you kind of got used to not really being sleepy. It's like being tired but your body keeps telling you, "I can't go no more, I can't do no more." But you still did it because you wanted to live. I'll be truthful, I fell asleep a few times. I tried to stay awake, wash down my eyes, slap myself.

Sometimes you just can't stay awake because you're so damned tired. At night, we had three guys on the gun squad, and each had half-hour watches. So we'd sleep three hours, then be on another hour and a half. But that's every night, seven days a week. I tried my best to stay awake.

I used to go out of my way to help those rookie guys who

were more tired than I was during watch. The guys I was with meant a lot to me. Everybody was real close to each other.

They would give us three boxes of C-rations for five days. That's if we were re-supplied on time. Those three boxes of C-rations are one meal each. There were times that we went on operations and we didn't stop to eat. Sometimes the action was so heavy that food was the last thing on your mind. But I think water was the most important. A lot of times we'd run out of water. They taught us survival skills, like breaking out some plastic and putting a cup on the bottom and try to get the moisture, but we never had time for none of that. We were supposed to get Sunday packages every Sunday which had candy, sodas, beer, and all this other stuff. But we seldom got them.

We'd go a lot of days without taking a bath. About the only time we really got to take a bath out in the bush was when we were crossing a river, and we'd dip ourselves with everything on. One thing happens after you dry out. Your body heat starts coming out and your clothes start drying. That's when that rotting sensation starts coming in. Most of the time, your crotch will be the first place that will rot. They used to tell us not to sit on hot rocks because you'd get hemorrhoids.

The part that really stands out is the winter time, the monsoon season. That stands out more than anything else. When we would climb the mountains it was so slippery that for every step you take up, it'd seem as if you had taken two down. Once you got to the top it was cool because the first guy would make a trail by putting his ass on the ground and slide down and hope that he didn't hit a branch or root. With the weight of your gear it was difficult to get up once you fell down.

Every place we went to we had to make a hole. I remember one instance, we made seven holes in seven days. There were other times that we'd move ten klicks in one day. One particular time, the choppers couldn't come to pick us up because of the monsoon. At this time, we were moving day and night. Night time is the worst time. The thing they didn't tell us was that there was a batallion of gooks behind us. We had guys who were refusing to move anymore because during the monsoon season you get a lot of that cellulitis-jungle rot. I still have a little jungle rot on my right leg. It always comes out in the summer time, I get little blisters. One guy had it and his feet got pink and his outside skin was dissolving-like. We took his boots off and put T-shirts and whatever we could arrange on his feet so that he could walk. He gave up, threw his 16 and broke it. He told his guys, "That's it. I'm not going anymore." Guys passed him up. Every time we'd slow down, we'd see him back there. They didn't give us any chance to stop. We had a lot of guys who were refusing to move anymore. But once they told us there was a batallion of gooks behind us, we began to move again.

You can only go so far when they push you to your limits. Actually, I was way past my limits by then. In the beginning, all they had to do was tell us that, and it would have straightened a lot of things out. But they waited until they found out how far we could go.

We believed that they were after us because we had hit the shit hard enough that instead of standing our ground, we were the ones who left. We were the ones who split. The NVA kicked our asses that day. It was a big operation. We had Koreans, ARVN's, Australians and New Zealanders with us on this operation. We hit a lot of shit and instead of us going forward, we caught ourselves going backwards.

There was one guy who had a big boulder fall on him and it crushed him to death. We were walking down a hill when someone above let loose a rock and it hit that guy. We put the dead guy in a body bag when the chopper came to pick him up. The guy with the jungle rot was put on a stretcher and the chopper took off with the guy still hanging on the stretcher. The ARVN's had no backbone, they had no pride in themselves. They would stay with you if you were kicking the enemy's ass. They'd book quick if we weren't kicking ass. We didn't have any place to go. We had to follow the system. They could just take off, run into the jungle and they'd be gone. I didn't like the ARVN's. I wouldn't go out of my way to help an ARVN.

I fought a lot of NVA. They were well organized and a good army. We were better. But I only think we were better because we had fire support, artillery, jets, choppers, and they didn't. We were bigger and stronger, but they had more patience than we did. I hated them. That was because they'd kill your buddies and you got a taste for them. You'd try to do them in wrong. You'd want to cut and tear them up. You don't just want to shoot them; you want to get even, fuck the body up, you might say. Sometimes the NVA would still be alive when we got to them, and a lot of the guys would kick them in the head and bust their skulls open.

When we'd catch POW's, sometimes they would have a rifle with no stock on it, just the barrel and the trigger, and they could shoot you right between the eyes. If you'd give them an M-14, they could have fired more deadly.

At first you're scared, but after awhile the *susto* seems to go away. You will find that your fright will make you do things that you don't think you can do. Once you get past that, everything else just becomes a reflex, it's more of not thinking and just doing it. The longer you go into your tour, the sharper you get.

There were a few times we had to make our trail backwards. One morning I woke up and the guy we had on watch wasn't really looking out. He didn't see all these heads popping up all of a sudden. All we did was grab what we could and try to fight. There were too many heads (NVA) on one side, so we started backing up. As the unit started running back, my M-60 happened to be among the last people on the line. I fired a few rounds to slow the NVA down. I remember feeling a concussion and I didn't really feel anything hit, but I kept running. I jumped over a log and caught up with some of my guys. The first thing I did was reach for my ass because I thought that's where it hit me. What happened was that the concussion blew a hole through my pants, and I got hit with small shrapnel. I didn't want to look at first because I thought my cheeks were gone. There was a little blood there, but nothing to keep me from doing what I had to do.

I know it had to be one of our guy's grenades that hit me, but that's the way things happen out there. When I came home, I put on my civilian briefs and a little piece of shrapnel came off. I never reported it because I didn't want my mom to get a telegram from the Marines. That would have scared and worried her too much. So I never reported the wound.

I talked to the Man (God) a lot. My belief at that time was very strong. A lot of it was because of the situation. I had this thing about never feeling alone. You may think you're a million miles away, you're all by yourself, and nobody knows you're there. For some reason, there's always a man there who knows what you're doing. You get so scared, and you have no place to turn. So you always think about the Man, as your last hope. You've got prayers going out, " Oh please, I want to go home, please get me by this." But you're always thinking about it, I think everybody did. You get so scared that you got to hang on to something.

I thought about my mom a lot—my parents, which helped me out a lot. I didn't want my mom to suffer as far as me not coming back. The way I thought about it was, if I was going to come back, I would come back whole. If I wasn't, I wouldn't come home. When I first went overseas, the only thing I wanted to do was make my mom and dad proud of me. But as things went along, it seemed to fade away. It didn't become as important. What became more important was being able to get home safely.

When you're over there (Viet Nam), it's a high in itself. You figure that nobody can touch you, and that nobody could even hurt you. It's just a phase of emotions that you go through, everybody goes through, and you can't change them because they're there. The only thing is to forget about them and hope the ideas don't ever come back, because you're surprised at what a human body can do to another without even thinking about it. But only with the right reasons or the right surroundings can you do this. You just can't do it because you want to do it. You'd be a basket case. You'd be in trouble. Civilization and culture are made so you aren't supposed to go around blowing people up. It's like getting mad and wanting to kill the person right away. And that's what we did in Viet Nam.

The government gave us a job to do. Which, for me, went beyond all of my beliefs. I was brought up to believe not to hurt anyone else. Here they give you an open invitation to do anything you want to. The guy doesn't have to be pointing the gun at you to snuff him out. You can do it if you want to, it's right there. You get a high out of it. Or you can get a bad taste of it and it can be hard to get rid of if you go too far.

We got away with a lot of things because everybody else was doing it. They'd give us an area and tell us to search and destroy. Nothing comes out, no POW's, no nothing. What they were telling us when we went into that area is nothing comes out of there except you. We used to waste villagers, but we did it at a distance so we didn't have to see the person looking at us. That would stick in your head. We'd open up with everything we had and yet, a lot of them would get away. They would send us into areas we had already been, and we'd know it was hot. When we went back in that area, if anything moved we'd let them have it because we didn't have the time to think, "Is it friendly or not?"

At the beginning I thought I was fighting for my country. I went with an open mind. I did what I was told. But as it went along, I found out I was lied to in just about everything. They wouldn't tell you anything they didn't want you to know. Sometimes they would tell us a place is not hot and it was. They'd send us to areas we had already been through and had kicked ass, then they would give it back to the enemy. Just like they did the whole country of Viet Nam. That never made any sense to me, and it still doesn't. As I went along further, I got a bitter taste, opposite of what I went there for. I went over there proud and I came back disappointed and unrespectful.

I caught malaria, then I caught typhoid fever, then I caught malaria again. The first time I got malaria I went to a sanctuary for thirty days. For the typhoid, I went to the Philippines, then to Guam for a couple of months. I got the typhoid from drinking bad water. When I was in Guam, a navy doctor told me I was unfit for infantry duty and that I was going back to the States. But somewhere along the line, he was overruled and I was sent back to Nam. Then I caught malaria again. But the malaria I caught would only hit me at night. All they told me was if I let my resistance go down, it could hit me hard again. For malaria we were supposed to get a white pill every day and a bigger pill on Sundays. Well, we were lucky if we got one on Sunday. We didn't get one everyday. There were a lot of things we were supposed to get that we didn't know about. That's the part I don't understand about the military. They have such high standards and yet they don't follow through on their part of the standard.

Our platoon was about sixty percent minority—Chicanos, Blacks, Puerto Ricans and Indians. We had one Puerto Rican, Reyes. He was a bad motherfucker. This guy was born to fight, he ate it up. He received the bronze star, silver star and the purple heart. He caught tuberculosis and was sent home. I found that the Mexicans had more pride in themselves and in doing a job, no matter what job it was. They seemed to have the quality of finishing what they started and doing the best that they could. I saw *gabachos* break down and give up. All the Chicanos I saw, whether they'd be from Texas, Arizona or wherever, had a lot of pride in themselves. Now, the Puerto Ricans were made to fight. Those guys are tight. If you get on their wrong side, you're in trouble; but if you get on their good side, they will stand by you. They are good people. This guy Monte, a black guy from Kentucky, was ready to fire up this staff sergeant. He was going to snuff him out. I got a chance to talk him out of it. I told him, "Let's go party." Most of these problems occurred in the rear areas.

The Viet Nam War was political. It was the United States butting into somebody else's business and trying to be a good Joe about it. The U.S. was trying to get other countries to think of them as good people, when they really didn't belong there in the first place. I look at it in the way that if it's their fight, let them fight it themselves. We ain't got no business fighting over there. We were fighting a country clear across the world and we didn't get nothing out of it. I think the United States lost in the political and military sense. The United States killed more of theirs than they killed of ours because the United States was much better equipped than the enemy. If the enemy had been equipped with just tanks and choppers, that war would have been completely different.

Right before I was supposed to go home, I got into a fight. But the fight really was all the frustrations I had built up and they all came out. We were drinking in a Da Nang bar, and we had been doing some dope. We took some kind of pills and drank them down with everything from 151 rum to champagne; we drank it all. It was me, Martinez from Sanger, and Art Flores from Texas, who were partying together. I remember that they threw us out of the bar. We were going back to our base when we passed the White Elephant Hotel. There was an ARVN unit to the side of the hotel. There was an ARVN guard on duty and we started fucking with him. Anyways, the dude took the safety off his rifle. I was on his right hand side and I pulled the rifle off of him, I swung back and the fiberglass butt broke on his face. The next thing I knew there was a bunch of gooks who started jumping on us. We started to throw them all over the place. Somehow we ended up in front of the hotel, and then in the hotel lobby. I remember they got me in a corner and they were kicking the shit out of me. I reached over and got one of those big water bottles and busted a dude with it.

The dude went down and was bleeding all over the place.

I had my back turned and was outside by then, and somebody grabbed my shoulder. It was an Army Sergeant Major and I broke his jaw. Somehow they got me back inside the deal, and they had Martinez outside. They got me back in the hotel and got me onto the balcony. I remember looking down, they had Martinez underneath the water buffalo fountain and he was full of sand, and they were just kicking the shit out of him. It was the Army MP's doing this. They told everybody to go inside, and I was still on top, so they told me to get my fucking ass inside. And I told them, "I'll go when I'm ready." They said, "You go inside now or we will put you inside." "Well, wait a minute," I told one of the MP's. I went downstairs and I hit the guy (MP). I don't remember much except that they beat me up bad. They kicked the shit out of me.

I woke up in a connex box. They had me handcuffed on my ankles and my wrists behind my back. They took my belt and my shoelaces. I was laying there all bruised up. I was throwing up big time, too. I could see the little holes on top of the connex box and it was hotter than shit. I began kicking the box and I told them, "Hey, you can't hold me here. I'm going back to the States." I was laying on my left side and puking. I couldn't get away from the puke that came out. I'll never forget the bad smell. The connex box was about four by four and by nine o'clock in the morning it was about 103 degrees.

They let me out of the connex box in the afternoon. From there they took me to the brig. I got a chance to talk to an army lawyer. He made a lot of smart remarks. He didn't really give a shit. He had a job to do and he just wanted to get it out of the way. They sent me and Martinez back to Quang Tri. Flores had somehow gotten away from the MP's during the scuffle. We ended up staying in country two extra months because the court-martial came around by that time.

After they sent us back to Quang Tri, all we did was stand guard with all the new guys. We would make the new guys stay awake all night while we slept. To me, I figured I was in a secure area compared to being out in the bush. I used to tell them to wake me up if they saw some movement, but otherwise not to wake me up at all.

All I did was party those two months. I got fucked up every day and every night. When they came to pick us up for the court-martial, me and Martinez were all fucking out of our heads. They gave us new fatigues and jungle boots and the whole bit. When we went in front of the board to get court-martialed, we were all fucked up, too. We didn't give a shit. We knew that they weren't going to do nothing to us.

They wanted me to apologize to the guy whose jaw I broke. I said, "No, I ain't apologizing to this guy because he grabbed me. It was self-defense." "Well then, you're going to pay the consequences," the head judge told me. "Well, fuck it then," I thought. "What are they going to do? Send me to Nam? I'm already here." He knew I didn't give a shit. He just got what he could out of it. So they busted us from corporal (E-4) to private first class (E-2), and a fine of one month's pay at ninety dollars a month. It didn't bother me at all. I knew I was going home one time or another.

When I got back to the United States, they didn't let us go home right away because it took two weeks to process us out. It was early in the morning when we got to California and they let us call home. As soon as we could, we all ran to the telephones. I called my mom and dad and it was a very touchy thing. All I could think of was, "I'm getting out of this place now." I took off about two days later. I went home. I never got caught because I had someone answer here to my name in the morning formations. I wasn't the only one doing it. There must've been twenty-five to thirty guys missing from the ranks.

I was glad I came home alive. But I am hurt because of the fact that I have to live with the things I did and they're going to be in my memory the rest of my life. The things that I saw myself do, I ain't proud of. For a long time, I thought God was punishing me by letting me see myself as a different person. I went through a lot of shit, both physically and mentally. I really can't believe some of the things I saw and did. I know what I did and I am stuck with them, but I ain't proud of them. I snuffed seventeen dudes out, and I can remember all seventeen of them.

THE MILITARY SHAFT

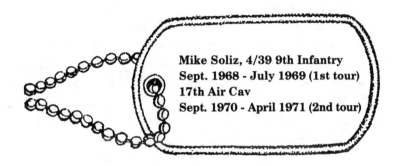

Mike Soliz, 4/39 9th Infantry
Sept. 1968 - July 1969 (1st tour)
17th Air Cav
Sept. 1970 - April 1971 (2nd tour)

A ll I knew about Viet Nam was that I was going to have a rifle and that I was going to be shooting at people, the enemy. The idea of maybe not making it back didn't even cross my mind until I got there. That's when I found out that I might not get back (home). When I went over there, I thought I was going to be the only one doing any firing and that no one was going to fire back at me. I thought this was so because we were superior, you know, the good guys. I figured that I would be over there two or three months before we won the war.

At the time I got to Viet Nam, our company was working off river boats on the Mekong River. During the day we stayed on the boats, when it got dark we would leave the boats for land in order to set up night ambushes. We'd walk, oh, maybe two miles away from the boats and set up the night ambush positions. The boats were pretty secure because of the big guns that the boats had, and clearings that the construction crews had made, made it difficult for the enemy to fire upon

85

the boat. Besides that, there were land patrols all around the boat at all times. We never did get bothered while we were on the boats. Once we got on land, it was a different story all together.

One of the things I couldn't understand was why our unit, out in the field, was eighty percent minorities: Blacks, Chicanos, Indians and Puerto Ricans. It seemed like it was the minorities who were always the infantry guys and the other people (whites) who had the rear jobs, maintenance, clerks and desk jobs. I got to see plenty of that over there.

I got to meet a lot of Chicanos over there. They were from all over, but the majority of them were from Texas, California, New Mexico and Arizona. My whole squad was made up of Chicanos. I also met some Indians. Most of them were from the Dakotas and Minnesota. They even spoke Indian amongst themselves. I was even stupid enough to ask them if they still lived in tepees.

The first time you make contact is the one that you can't forget. You might forget the other fire fights and ambushes, but not the first one. That's the one I remember the most because I had never been shot at in all of my life. We lost some twenty-two guys in one fire fight. We got caught in what is called a horseshoe ambush. They caught us off guard because we never thought that they would be there because we were pretty close to a big village. We didn't think the Viet Cong would be there. We never even saw them, we never had a chance. They let our whole company walk into the ambush. To pull an ambush like that requires a lot of men. I lost two good friends in that ambush. I hadn't known them for very long, but over there you make good friends quick.

We were so close to the village, actually, it was a town, that we could hear the children playing. They caught us off guard because the VC used the village as a decoy. They knew that the Americans would not fire at a village. We were told to keep the civilians out of the action. But, who were the civilians and who were the Viet Cong? Our company barber back at

Dong Tam, the division base camp, was killed in an ambush. He was a Viet Cong. We kept saying to ourselves how many times had that guy had a razor and shaved us. To me he was 45 to 50 years old, and I could never figure out why he was always asking us questions. He would ask us about personal things, then he would ask when we were moving out and things like that. Everybody really got to like him.

We had a little boy taking us sodas everywhere we went. That little kid always seemed to be around. One time he caught us off guard, too. He paddled his little boat down a narrow canal until he reached us on the side of the bank. He would carry bags full of sodas, and we would trade him the sodas for our C-rations. One time he left one of those bags there. He said we could have it and nobody paid any attention to it. It was a command detonated mine is what it was. Command detonated mine means that this kid left it and it was detonated from a distance. It killed two soldiers. Bam! Just like that.

We didn't know who the enemy was. There were times that we even caught the South Vietnamese Army shooting at us. We were supposed to be helping them fight the North Vietnamese. It was kind of hard to figure out.

One thing I couldn't understand was Christmas truces. I could not believe that. I'll never forget one incident when they wanted to court-martial this colored guy. Bob Hope had come to Dong Tam. He had Ann Margaret and a whole bunch of other stars with him. So they set this seventy-two hour Christmas truce. We were told that we couldn't fire our weapons for nothing, at nobody. We didn't get to see the show because it was our company's turn to be on patrol. It was late in the afternoon when we could actually see them (VC) walking with their black fatigues and their AK-47's. They knew we couldn't shoot at them. That's when I told the Lieutenant, "Sir, that guy over there who we're letting go, when this truce is over, he could be the same guy who's going to kill me. Shouldn't I kill him first, now?" Then he says, "Soliz, we're not fighting a war, we're fighting politics. We were told not to fire, so we can't fire."

That's when this colored kid from Jackson, Mississippi, got in trouble. We were setting up to go out that night, and he was an ammo bearer for one of the machine guns. They wanted him to strap down with something like three or four hundred rounds of machine gun ammo. He said he was not going to take anything. Why should he take it if we weren't going to fire it? He didn't take it. The captain threatened to court martial him for disobeying a direct order. He said, "I don't care what you do. I'm not going to take something if I'm going to have the enemy laugh at me for carrying all this stuff."

When we got back to camp the MP's came and took him. I never found out what happened to him, but I think he was court-martialed and sent to the stockade.

One time we were told to go on a search and destroy mission. Our captain told us to shoot at anything going faster than a walk, because once we'd get there the Viet Cong would start running. We walked into the village and asked the men for their ID's. Whoever didn't have an ID was Viet Cong. That's why the CO said to kill anything going faster than a walk. What we did was pick a couple of squads to go into the village to ask for ID's. At the same time, the rest of the troops were put in position around the village to make sure nobody ran out. When they ran, they ran straight into the other soldiers. We caught eleven VC that day. We caught them off guard and without their weapons. That's about the only search and destroy mission I was on because I probably spent more time in the hospital than I did in the bush.

During the monsoon season there was so much rain that we couldn't get resupplied for five or six days. We'd get hungry. We used to get together about five or six Chicanos and just look at each other and say who's going to eat the first one. We used to catch the rodents in the rice paddies with our steel pots. They'd be running in the paddies. They were big suckers—big rats. We just had to cook them and eat. *Hijola* man, once they were cooked they were good.

I remember an *Indio* named Soledad. He would eat snakes before he would eat C-rations. He'd just peel the *cuero* off of it, chop it into pieces and cook it over the fire just like you cook marshmellows. *Asina*—he'd eat them there, just like that. I asked him how he could be eating that. He told me, "We eat that all the time; it's good meat. Taste." "No, thank you," I'd tell him. When those guys got together, they would speak in their own language. They were Plains *Indios*.

One time we were out in the boonies for about three months. We had nothing but C-rations to eat and no mail call for a long time. I'll never forget this one day when they brought in a chinook and brought everybody a warm meal. *Hijola,* I'll never forget that.

And then it started to rain. This was the monsoon season. After we had finished eating, our CO told us, "Gentlemen, we haven't received no mail call in a while, so I made it a point that they are going to drop mail. I don't care what kind of weather we're having, but we're going to get the mail today."

When the chopper with mail came in, it was pouring like hell and it couldn't land. So what they did was put the mail in plastic bags and dropped it. It so happened that it was dropped in the river. And the river was really swollen. Boy! Martinez dived in the water trying to get the mail. He was going full blast until he got it. The funniest thing about it was that he didn't get one letter.

We would have never known that he didn't get any mail until he told us himself. What everybody did was put their ponchos over themselves because it was pouring. Martinez didn't even do that. He just sat on his helmet and you could see all the water running down on him. That's when I asked him, "What's wrong?" "*Nada*," he said. "Then why are you so serious... did they leave you or what?" "No, if it was like that, it would be all right... at least I would have gotten a letter."

Everybody got some mail. I got nine letters by myself. I told him, "Hey, Martinez, here you can read one of mine." "You know what," he said, "I feel like a big dummy, I looked like the pony express ... the mail comes through." Everybody began to crack up at him, poor dude. He sat all by himself. A little bit afterwards I went over and talked to him. "You know," he said, "I could have drowned out there for you bastards. I could have been shot if there had been some Viet Cong on the bank. I didn't even get one piece of mail. When I get home—that's what we called our base camp—I'm going to write home and I'm going to chew out some people. This is embarrassing."

When we got back to our base camp about four days later he looked real sad ... we were on stand-down. That's when I asked him, "Write any letters today?" "No," he said, "*Yo no voy a escribir hasta que no me escriban.*" I told him. "If they haven't written to you in three months. You aren't going to get any." I made a mistake in telling him, "You know what, if I were you, I'd kill myself right now. What's the matter, doesn't your family know how to write or what?"

Every once in a while we'd run into a village where they had these night women. Those places were off limits. You get caught there and you're automatically court-martialed. We went into one of these villages that had those ladies and two colored guys went to see them. I guess they couldn't take it anymore. We set about a hundred yards from the village. In the daytime they'd come up to us and advertise what they were doing. Those two took off and never came back. As far as I know, those guys are still missing in action. The next day when we were ready to take off, the sergeant was asking about those two guys and nobody said nothing. It didn't surface until about two or three weeks later when some of their own people revealed that they had taken off to where the women were. After that got around, nobody was going to go out there. When I found out about that, I said to myself, I don't need it that bad. I'll wait for R&R.

I never made it to an R&R. I always got wounded before I had a chance to. I didn't really know how I got out so lucky. I was the third man from the point. A booby trap killed the first two guys, wounded me, and killed the next three guys behind me. It was a command detonated mine. I had a total of a hundred and sixty-two stitches on the back of my legs, that's where the majority of the shrapnel hit me. It took me ninety-seven days to recuperate at Camp Zama, Japan.

I didn't feel nothing until I was in the hospital. I was knocked out for three days. I didn't even feel the helicopter ride out of there. I didn't even feel when they put me on the stretcher. The next thing I knew I was in the Third Medi-Vac in Saigon. I couldn't believe I was out for three days and that I had been operated on. I was there for eleven days, and they told me that it would be a while before I would walk again. They were thinking of bringing me to the States, but since I had only been in country for three months—it was like she said—"If you would have been in country over six months, we wouldn't hesitate to send you to the States." That counted because they wanted you to go back and do it again, to get their money's worth, in other words.

So, she told me I was going to Japan. I was all for it, just get me out of here. The next morning they woke me up about three o'clock in the morning for the C-141 flight. There must of been about six of us on litters, which means we had to be carried out. I had to have a nurse go on the flight with me because my legs would bleed all of the time. It was beautiful country up there. The hospital was nice and so were the Air Force personnel.

One day Camp Zama was playing basketball against another unit. That's when I saw Richard Ramos from Corcoran playing basketball. A couple of the guys had pushed my wheelchair to the gym. As I was watching the game, I said to myself, "That guy looks familiar." Then all of a sudden he comes over and walks around and says, "Mike?" I answered, "Yeah." "Remember me?" "I think I do now," I said. I saw him often until I left the hospital. Sometimes they wouldn't let me go to the basketball games because they wanted me confined to bed.

They took care of me 24 hours a day. I would wake up at four in the morning and by seven o'clock I had eaten breakfast and was ready to start my therapy sessions. They gave me therapy three times a day. By Easter Sunday I was on my way back to Viet Nam.

When I got back in country I was sent to the Ninth Replacement to be processed. I was waiting in one of the barracks when these guys came up and told me that I was leaving for Dong Tam in two days. The last night I was there, I was in bed when I heard someone playing a guitar and singing. It was coming from a far corner of the barracks. The light was dim, so it was hard to see who was playing. I thought to myself that that sounds like Richard Aguilar. Naw, I thought, what would Richard be doing way out here. As I was laying there he passed by and I said, "Rich." He said, "God." It was like a family reunion. Me and him had taken basic and AIT together. He had just returned from a Saigon hospital where he had been treated for shrapnel wounds. We went to the NCO Club and got good and drunk. I didn't see him again until we got back to the States. I was putting gas one day at a gas station in Hanford, and he happened to drive by with his girlfriend. He looked at me and told me, "I'm sure glad you made it back because I thought about you all that time I was over there."

When I got back to my unit I was gun-shy. What used to get us was the Mekong Delta. There were a lot of rice paddies and we were always wet. And during the monsoon we got even wetter. There were times when we would just sit out there with rain just hitting us. The mosquitos, bugs, and leeches didn't help either. We couldn't even sleep with all that rain. All that time I kept saying to myself, "What am I doing here?" We had a platoon leader who said it right. He said, "When you're here, you're like in another world. You have to forget what's back there, because if you don't, you're not going back there (home). If you've got your head up your ass, that's where it's going to stay, because you're not going to make it back."

There was this one guy who went as far as shooting his toes off. He did it during a fire fight and it couldn't be proved that he did it to himself. Another guy in another company shot his finger off with a 45 pistol.

When I first got in the country, I had the problem of snoring out in the bush. We were out on a night ambush. As I was sleeping, this real big *gabacho* taps me with his weapon. "Soliz," he said, "if you don't stop that fucking snoring, I'm going to blow you away right here. They'll (enemy) hear this shot, but they will only hear it one time. They won't hear you snoring all goddamn night. I'll blow you away, Soliz. I have a hundred and one days left and I intend to survive them." He said I stopped snoring. He was right in doing that because I was endangering myself and the rest of the soldiers.

It's like going to sleep on guard duty. I caught this one Puerto Rican guy sleeping on guard one night. That night we were real close to the VC because we could hear them laughing and we could also smell the pot that they were smoking. When I crawled to where he was at, he was asleep. I asked him in Spanish if he was asleep. He said that he wasn't, that he was just thinking. It was my responsibility to make sure everybody was awake that was supposed to be awake. "Don't go to sleep," I told him. When I came around he was not only asleep, but this time he was snoring. The next day when we went back to the camp, I told the Puerto Rican guy, "You know what? I can have you busted." What pissed me off was that he was arguing with me that he wasn't asleep. He just kept arguing and arguing with me. If the guy would have told me, yeah, OK, I was asleep. But he pissed me off so bad that I reported him.

He was endangering the rest of the guys. He was court-martialed and busted. He swore that wherever we met, he was going to get even with me. I had him transferred out of the platoon. I thought that maybe he would shoot me in the back or something. And, at the same time, what comes around, goes around. I was thinking I might get him first, so I thought it would be better for him to be transferred. He was killed a few months later. Why? For sleeping on guard.

I fell asleep on guard one time. We had walked about ten miles that day because they were supposed to pick us up by choppers but they couldn't pick us up. That night when I was on guard, I was yawning and this and that. The platoon sergeant came around and racked me on the side of the ribs with the butt of his rifle. He told me, "If you fall asleep one more time on guard duty, I'm going to blow your head off. We've got a lot of good men here," he told me. Sometimes you just couldn't stay awake because of just pure exhaustion.

One time a good friend of mine, Hector Moreno was his name, was almost killed because someone fell asleep on guard duty. They went out on a night ambush and they were attacked when they were all asleep. About fifteen of them had their throats slit with knives. Hector was one of the fortunate ones who woke up in time to see it all. I talked to him after the incident. He was never the same again. There were times when he would talk about exactly what had happened, and then all of a sudden he'd start yelling. He was sent home as a mental case.

One day we were on patrol and we had seen VC walking on the rice paddies. They saw us so they began to move into the jungle. I was ready to call artillery. The sniper fired just one shot. That's the one that got me. It got me behind my left shoulder. I went down to one knee and I felt a burning sensation. The guy just fired one shot, he didn't fire one more. I was leaning on a tree when the bullet ricocheted and hit me. If it hadn't ricocheted off the tree, the wound would have been much worse. This happened about three weeks after I had gotten back from Japan.

I was medevaced out back to Dong Tam. I couldn't move my arm. From there I was sent to Camp Zama. I was there for 22 days. One of the nurses I knew there didn't even know that

I had left and had returned. As soon as I recovered, I was sent back to Viet Nam. When I got back to Nam, I was on the other side of the mountain, I was getting short. By this time I was really getting scared. Damn, I thought, sooner or later I'm going to get killed.

One of the guys who I most remember getting killed was a guy who had just gotten there. I met him back at base camp and we began to talk as we were drinking a beer. He had just gotten there and he showed me his wedding pictures. He had only been there fourteen days when he got killed. He made the biggest mistake that can ever happen. We were on patrol and he was walking the rear. And I guess, he stopped to go to the bathroom because that's what one of the guys said that he had told him—that he would catch up as soon as he was done. We kept walking and walking until we stopped to set up our night position. Then someone said, "Where's the new guy?" He was nowhere around. The first sergeant said, "Well, he probably got scared and took off." The next day we were walking back the same way and we found him dead on the trail. The VC had been following us and they stabbed him to death. His name was Florencio Guzman from Amarillo, Texas.

I lost a real good friend of mine. That really tore me up. My oldest boy is named after him. *Se llamaba* James Thomas Woods, from Boon, North Carolina. We were like Heckel and Jeckel, we would go everywhere together. He's the one who showed me all the ropes. He was killed in ambush. I wasn't there when he was killed because I was in Japan. I've had some real good friends in my life, but there isn't one yet that can beat that guy as a friend. I wrote to his parents from Viet Nam. Even now, it's been almost twenty years, I tell my wife that I will visit his family one day. His father wrote back to me and told me that I was welcome in their house.

Twenty-seven days after I had gotten back from Japan, I was hit again. We were in a fire fight and I was shot in the side. Good thing the bullet hit me at such an angle that it didn't hit any organs. I thought that I was going back to Japan. They said since I could walk and move my hands, they'd send me to a hospital in Cam Rahn Bay instead.

I could not believe that Cam Rahn Bay was part of Viet Nam. It looked like some sort of exotic island somewhere else. That's when I first heard that my unit was going back to the States.

After I recovered I was sent back to my unit. When I got there the first sergeant told me that the company would be out in the field another six or seven days and that I could wait for them there in the company area. I couldn't understand why the first sergeant was being so nice to me. I found out when he told me, "You know what?" he told me, "you're going to get killed yet. That's too many times."

When my company moved out to the field, I went with them. About eighteen days later we were on patrol when a sniper shot me in the calf. It was more than one sniper, and two guys were killed. Our squad was almost always the one on the point position. I couldn't figure this out until the CO told me that was because our squad was the most experienced. From there I was sent back to Cam Rahn Bay. There I got really lucky; it was the turning point of my first tour. I had spent about thirty-two days recuperating when my break came around. I was sitting around when this sergeant E-7 came around and asked when I was due back to my unit. I told him I was due back in a couple of days. He asked me if I wanted a job around the hospital for awhile. He offered me a forty-five day job. "What about my unit?" I asked him. "Well, just tell them you're still recuperating. We need a NCO to be in charge of the hospital patients who are well enough to pull details." I was assigned to assign details.

It was nice. I had a regular bed to sleep in, hot chow, and the NCO Club was just a short distance away. It was about a week before my twentieth birthday when a liaison officer from the Ninth Division told me that our unit was going home. He asked me when I had come in country, and I told him the twelfth of September. He told me that I made the cut-off date and that I should get my fat ass back to my unit as soon as possible.

I went to talk to Lieutenant Bentley, the executive officer, about what the liaison officer had told me. "Mike," he said, "I'll find out about that for you." The next day he walked into my office and he said, "You got to get home quick because they're cutting people fast." I left that afternoon, back for Dong Tam.

When I got back to my unit, the first sergeant said he was glad that I made it back. He told me to go to processing to see if I was eligible to go back home with the unit. And sure enough, I was. It took me a couple of days to process in order to be ready to go back to the States.

When I arrived at the company area, the first sergeant wanted me to ride shotgun on a convoy that was going out. I told him, "No way. I've got two or three days left here and I'm going to make it." "Mike," he said, "You're just riding shotgun." I told him I had seen too many things "just" riding shotgun. I didn't go on it either.

In a couple of days after I got processed, we were airlifted by helicopter. It was something like seven thousand guys who were flown on chinook helicopters from Dong Tam to Saigon. Each one of those helicopters carries about sixty soldiers, so you can imagine how many choppers that took to fly us away. They wanted to send us in convoys but they didn't want to take a risk.

The soldiers that didn't make the breakoff day for time in country were reassigned to the Twenty-Fifth Infantry Division and the First Cavalry Division, because they were pretty close to our division area of operation. As I was riding the chinook, I was just hoping it wasn't shot down.

When we got to Saigon, I couldn't believe it. It was just too good to be true. But I wasn't going to be satisfied until the plane was up in the air. They had a parade for us there at the airport in Saigon. There were a lot of civilians that put wreaths of flowers around our necks. The commanding general was there. He came around and shook our hands and told us we had done a good job, and all of that. We didn't care about that, we just wanted to get on one of those Tiger Airline planes.

We finally boarded the plane and I just couldn't believe I was going home. Up in front of the plane was a big canvas, sort of like a curtain. We couldn't figure out what it was for. About two hours before we were to land at McChord Air Force Base, Washington they lifted the canvas. Behind it were cases of beer. The commanding general had put them there for us. By the time we landed at McChord Air Force Base, we were pretty well lit up.

When we landed, there must have been about fifteen thousand people who were waiting there for us. I'll never forget this one lady who had come down to greet her son. When we were getting off the plane, the band was playing and the crowd was cheering. Well, the MP's were there guarding so the people would not get too close to the plane. When she saw her son coming off the plane, she wanted to go to him. The MP's told her that she had to wait until later. She told them, "I'm not waiting for nobody. I flew down here and I've sat here three days waiting for my son. And I just saw my son over there, so get out of my way." She just walked past the MP's and went to hug her son.

I was on top of the world because I had made it home. I mean, I wasn't back in my home town yet, but heck, like one colored guy said, "I can walk home from here, and I live in New York City."

The people there were just as nice as possible. They stood there until all of the troops were off the planes. It only took three hours to process all of the troops. From the air base they took us to Fort Lewis. When we got to Fort Lewis, they told us we would be there for about seventy-two hours, and that the following morning we would be taken to downtown Seattle for a parade. That night they took us to the mess hall and gave us the biggest steak dinner I've ever had. They gave us an hour and a half of free phone calls. I had never seen so many phone booths in all of my life. From there I called my mom. After that, we were taken to one of the barracks to sleep.

The next morning we dressed in new jungle fatigues and went to Seattle for the parade. The Ninth Marine Division had also arrived by this time. One of the good things about being dressed in fatigues was that if the Marines had been dressed in their formal uniforms, they would have stood out. But they were dressed in fatigues too.

There were about one hundred thousand people at the parade. It was an exhilarating experience.

After the parade we went back to Fort Lewis where we received our orders. I had a few months to go in the army so I was sent to Fort Hood, Texas, for my next assignment. But before I was to report to Fort Hood, I was given a forty-six day leave.

As soon as they let me leave, I took a flight from Seattle to San Fransisco, then to Fresno. My cousin John and my brother Ruben picked me up at the airport in Fresno. They picked me up at four o'clock in the afternoon and we partied until three o'clock in the morning. We blew it because they were supposed to have a big party for me. Boy, was my fiancee mad at me! When we came home we were drunker than hell. I was so glad to see my family. My dad told me that Nancy, my fiancee, had been waiting for me to pick her up in Hanford since that afternoon.

The next morning my mother told me I was in hot water, and that Nancy had just called. "Oh! Nancy," I said. My mom said, "You haven't seen her in a year and you'd rather party with your friends than go and pick her up." So, I had John and Ruben take me to Hanford where they just dropped me off. Everything turned out right between me and her because we got married while I was on leave.

Everybody kept asking me the same questions; they

wanted me to talk about it. The first question they would ask was about the guys I had killed. They couldn't believe how many times I had been wounded. My brothers were the ones who asked me all these questions. I came back with a different attitude, I grew up, in other words. I knew what could happen, what would have happened, but didn't happen. I was glad to be one of the fortunate ones that made it. A lot of guys got killed over there.

When it was time to report to Fort Hood, Texas, my wife and I took a train. I'll never do that again. It took us four days to get there.

By the time I got to Fort Hood, I had seven months left in my military commitment. A few days after we got to Fort Hood, I told my wife that I had been offfered a four thousand dollar re-enlistment bonus and a job at Travis Air Force Base. I was supposed to instruct the Air Force people on basic orientation to combat in Viet Nam.

I thought it was a good deal. We would be a short distance from San Francisco and from our family in Corcoran and Hanford. My wife was all for it, and so was I. So, I did it. I bought a car, and they gave me a thirty day leave.

We came back to California for our leave. I told my mom and dad what I did. My mom didn't go for that. she said, "Son, why don't you just get out, you don't know what can happen. They might send you back to Viet Nam." "Mom," I told her, "they can't send me back, I just got here."

We went back to Texas after the leave. My wife was about in her eighth month of pregnancy with our first daughter when they called me into the office. The first sergeant told me he had some very interesting news for me. "Sergeant Soliz," he told me, "We just got a big levy come down, and they want mostly experienced guys from Viet Nam because too many young guys are getting killed." I said, "What does that got to do with me." "I hate to tell you this, but you're on this levy." I looked at him and I told him, "What! That can't be because I re-enlisted for the air defense command." "That doesn't make any difference because you're on this levy," he said. Oh! that pissed me off, so I went to the re-enlistment officer.

When I got to the re-enlistment officer, Staff Sergeant Martindale was his name, I asked him how this could have happened. "Soliz," he told me. "You got what they call in military terms—you got the military shaft. There isn't anything I can do." It was about two months before I was supposed to start my school. "I just got back from there, don't you see my records?" I told him. It wasn't his fault.

Coming home and telling my wife was the hardest part, especially since she was already pregnant. I got home in the afternoon, and I had bought a six pack. And I told her, "You know what, ah, I'm in trouble, we're in trouble." "Why are we in trouble?" she said. I said, "I've got to go overseas again." "Can't I go with you?" she asked. She was thinking I was going to Germany, Korea, or some place like that. "Where I'm going, you can't go," I told her. "You're not going back to Viet Nam?" she asked. I said, "Yes."

Oh! you should have heard her. She cried for two or three days straight. She cried and cried and cried. Finally, she asked me when we could go home. "I'll be leaving here in thirty days, but in thirty days you won't be able to go home because the baby will be due. What I'm going to do is take you home now." She didn't want to. I asked for a six day leave for the purpose of taking my wife home. We had to fly home because she was too far gone in her pregnancy.

The saddest part was when I got back to Texas. I had to stay there another thirty days. I felt so lonely on the flight to Texas. After the thirty days came around, I was allowed a fifteen day leave before I was to report to Oakland.

I met my brother Ruben in Oakland. Ruben was going to Viet Nam too. Me and my brother were talking in the mess hall when this guy told us that two brothers were not supposed to be in Viet Nam at the same time. I didn't know Ruben was supposed to go to Viet Nam because he didn't get a leave before he was to leave for Viet Nam. They sent him right out of training because they were going to Viet Nam as a unit. He asked us if we had both volunteered for Viet Nam. We told him that we hadn't. "Well, then," he said, "both of you can't go over there." He advised us to go see the Chaplain.

The afternoon before I was to leave for Viet Nam, they called us into the office. "There has been a mistake made," they told us. "You know the army makes mistakes." "Only one of you guys can go to Viet Nam," the lieutenant told us. "One of you will go to Viet Nam and the other one will go to Korea."

That's when Ruben said, "Since you've been to Viet Nam, you'll go to Korea and I'll go to Viet Nam." "No," I said, "you'll go to Korea and I'll go to Viet Nam." The reason was because I was Sergeant E-6 and he was a new guy, and they were going to put him right in the front lines. I thought to myself, if something were to happen to him I don't think I could ever live with knowing that I had had the chance to keep him alive. Anyway, since I was an E-6 and this my second tour, I thought I was going to get an easy rear job. We both talked about it, and I went to Viet Nam and he went to Korea. Up to this day no one knew about this besides me and him, not even my wife.

I went back to Cam Rahn Bay. From there I was assigned to the Seventh of the Seventeenth Air Cavalry, which was attached to the Americal Division. Camp Halloway was the base camp for that unit. When the first sergeant back in Texas told me about the levy, he said that I would probably be assigned to a nice rear job—but I wasn't.

When I reported to my company, the captain said, "Sergeant Soliz, you're here just in time. You're going to be in charge of the first rifle platoon." I looked at him with disbelief. I told him I thought I was going to get a rear job. He told me that maybe that's what they had told me back in the States, but that I was in Viet Nam now.

When I went to the platoon I was assigned to, some of the guys had told me that a couple of guys had gotten killed a few days earlier. I began to think, this time I'm going to die. We went out about three days after I got there. Our platoon leader, Lieutenant Miester, told me, "I'll tell you what Mike, you tell me what to do." He knew that I had a lot of experience and he didn't. He told me he had just volunteered our platoon for a mission. I told him, "Sir, that's the first thing you're not supposed to do, do not volunteer for anything like that." "Oh," he said, "I thought that we were supposed to look as if we were doing something." "Sir," I told him, "I can go back there (rear) and be in the mess hall eating or writing a letter to my wife, or I can think of a whole bunch of things I can do in the rear. If you want me to, Sir, I can go back to the rear and dig the latrine for the whole company." "Are you sure?" he said. Then I picked up my shirt and I showed him my wounds and I told him, "I know." Me and him got real close.

When we went back to Camp Halloway, we were there for sixty-two days without going out on patrol. We pulled a lot of guard duty and details. One day I saw him in the mess hall eating. I waited until the rest of the officers left to go and speak to him. "Sir," I asked him, "how come we ain't going out on patrol?" "Goddamn it, Mike, I don't understand you. You told me not to volunteer us for nothing. Don't you like it back here?" I said, "That's all I wanted to find out. We can do a whole year back here if we have to." "Yeah, but I want to learn," he said. "Sir, you're not going to be learning if you're dead." "Is it that bad?" he asked. "It's that bad, sir," I replied.

One day we had to go on a company size mission. That's when I got wounded again. A sniper hit me in the leg. When I was hit I couldn't move. There were a couple of Chicanos who I thought were my friends and they didn't help me. It was a black guy that picked me up in a fireman's carry and carried me to safety.

They sent me back to Cam Rahn Bay. I was there in the

hospital for about twenty-three days. After that I was sent back to Camp Halloway. I spent another two months pulling detail and making out the duty roster. I was getting bored and time was dragging. About this time the CO came around and asked me if I wanted to go on R&R. He came back three weeks later and told me I could go to Hawaii.

That's when I got wounded for the last time. I got shot maybe thirteen days before I was to go on R&R. It was a sniper again. This time I was sent to the hospital in Saigon. When I got there, a black female lieutenant colonel doctor looked at my medical records and she said, "Your war days are over for you boy, it's over, you're going home. They can't expect you to win the war by yourself. You've been wounded too many times."

I was sent back to the States from there. I wasn't even allowed to go back to my unit and pick up my stuff. From Saigon I was taken to Letterman Hospital in San Francisco. After I recuperated from my wound, I was sent home for a convalescence leave. I was told to wait at home for my orders telling me where to report.

They never sent me my orders. I waited so long for my orders that I even got a job at Gilkey Farms. I waited for three years. My mom kept telling me that I should go to Fort Ord and report. I told her that there was no reason to.

One day this FBI guy came to the house and asked me if I was AWOL from the army. Jimmy, my oldest boy, was about three years old. You know, sometimes he has asked me why I had to name him after a white boy. I told him because that's what my best friend's name was in Viet Nam—James Woods—and that he had gotten killed over there. Anyway, I asked the FBI guy why? Was I AWOL from the Army? And I showed him my orders. "Can you show where I've got orders telling me where I have to report to next?" "Why didn't you ever report to ask what was going on?" he said. "They told me to sit here and wait, and I'm waiting." "I can't believe that," he said, "they never sent you orders?"

He gave me two days to report back to Fort Ord. I went to Fort Ord, and wy wife was upset. She had told the FBI guy, "You aren't going to do it to him again." I spent about twenty-one days there before they discussed me.

I had to go to what they called a general court-martial. They threatened to punish me for being AWOL, but when I said I would get me a lawyer, they changed their tone. The commanding general told the court there wasn't anything that said that I was AWOL.

My father wanted me to get a lawyer in order to get my back pay. I said, "Dad, I don't want to push the issue. I got lucky this time. I made a mistake one time and re-enlisted. I think this time I screwed them, and I'm going to leave it like that. They had even given me a chance to get out of the army or to stay in with all of my rank and back pay. I was already settled at home, and decided I had had enough of the army and went back home.

THE BUSH

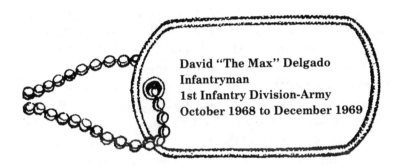

David "The Max" Delgado
Infantryman
1st Infantry Division-Army
October 1968 to December 1969

I stayed about five days at the San Francisco International Airport. I lived up there at the USO lounge. I couldn't make up my mind whether I should go to Canada or not. I was thinking it over but I finally decided against it because I didn't have the connections and my wife was waiting to hear from me. About the fifth day, the MP's were going around looking for people who were late to report to Oakland. That's when I decided to report to Oakland. When I got to Oakland, they didn't charge me nothing. They said it was OK. I guess they just needed guys to take the dead soldiers' places.

As soon as they opened the door, a heat wave came into the plane. That was my first taste of Viet Nam. They put us on a cattle truck and took us to a replacement center. I stayed there for a few days. I still couldn't believe I was there. I was horny as hell. I was thinking about women all the time. I couldn't believe I wasn't going to fuck for a long time.

I thought I was going to get killed, I swear to God. Every time I got in a fire fight or in trouble, I always prayed for my mom. My mom is dead, she died when I was a kid in the eighth grade. I used to carry a bible in the pocket of my jacket all of the time. Every time I got in trouble, I'd call out for mama—mom, mom help me out, I used to say. It worked, I guess, because here I am.

We'd stay out in the jungle most of the time. We'd sleep out in the jungle and put out ambushes. If no ambush came, we'd pick up our claymore mines and walk around again until we set another ambush. Once in a while, we'd blow an ambush. We'd blow it and start shooting our rifles *en chinga.* After that, we'd hear a lot of moaning from the gooks because they were all shot up. Then somebody would volunteer—not me—to put the guys out of their misery. There was a Puerto Rican guy who used to wear a jungle hat with one side of the brim pulled up like one of those Australian guys. He'd usually shoot the gooks to put them out of their misery. This didn't happen everyday but often enough that you couldn't forget what you did.

Maybe about two or three times a month we'd get into a fire fight or blow an ambush. It was always boring. You'd walk in the jungle and nothing would happen. If you saw something, you'd call for artillery. Then we would start walking again. We'd sit down and open our cans of meat and drink water. Then it'd get dark and we'd do the same thing all the time. I remember eating those C-rations, and they were delicious because I was hungry, and cool water to drink it down with felt real good. We didn't talk very much, but you think a lot. You open your rucksack and see the pictures of the house back home. It's kind of hard to masturbate out in the jungle. You're an animal out in the jungle.

We were setting up an ambush and digging in. The gooks were walking in the day time. It kind of surprised us. They heard us and started shooting at us. We hit the ground and started shooting back. There were some trees behind us and a gook shot a rifle grenade at me. It exploded on a tree and the shrapnel hit my back and part of my right nut. God! It hurt. I was all *escamado,* we were being attacked. Somebody told me, "Hey Delgado, you're hit! You're hit!" I didn't feel like I was hit because I was all *escamado,* but I had blood all over my back. The fire fight ended and the choppers came in. I was told to go in with the choppers.

In the hospital they took off my pants *y la chingada.* They took some shrapnel off my right nut, I think they took a piece of my nut off. Then they took the shrapnel off my back and legs. One of my cheeks still has a piece of metal in it. I can still feel it. That's part of war. I was in the hospital two weeks when they saw that I could walk. They told me to go back to my unit. They didn't care. As long as you can walk and carry a rifle and your name is Delgado, you go back to the jungle.

One time we were walking and we hit a base camp. They started shooting at us and we hit the ground. This guy was shooting at us with a machine gun. This was about, maybe, my second month in country. At first, I didn't know why everyone was hitting the ground. Some of them were falling from bullet wounds. "Delgado, Delgado, bring the gun up, bring the gun up," they said. I was about four or five *vatos* behind the front line. There were some bomb craters in front of us. "OK," I said, "I'm coming." I didn't think nothing of it. I crawled up about forty feet and set my M-60 machine gun up in front of the crater. I wasn't into it yet, I was just shooting the gun to the front and they told me I was setting real good crossfire. There was so much jungle there you couldn't see the fucking gooks, all you hear is them shooting at you. I had my head down when I was shooting. There was no way I was going to put my head up. I got a bronze star for that.

The gunships came and the artillery was called in. In about five or ten minutes, it was all over with. We went in to check out where we had hit. There was blood all over. I guess they had a fire going and they were going to eat rice because there was rice right there. With all the firepower they were hit with (jets, gunships and artillery), yet we hardly found any dead bodies. They must've carried their dead away because we found blood. They had sandals and AK forty-sevens, and they kicked our fucking ass. About the only time we ever found any dead bodies was when they would attack our base camp. They would attack about four o'clock in the morning and we would find some dead bodies along our perimeter.

When I first came in country, I was supposed to go with two other guys outside the perimeter as LP's, but they couldn't find me because I was on a detail. They put this one *mayate* who had come in country with me to take my place. At about four in the morning we got attacked with mortars and small-arms fire. The three LP's were killed. One of those guys could have been me. They figured it might of been us who killed them when they (LP's) were coming back to our perimeter. It wasn't me though, because I was on the other side of the perimeter. I never got the story straight because I also heard that they might have been killed with a grenade thrown by the gooks. It was all crazy, all confusion.

This happened about the first month I was there. There were two *mayates* and one *gabacho* who got killed on that LP. One of the *mayates*, Burdon, was my good friend. After that, I was kind of getting used to it. I didn't care if I was wearing the same old fatigues or anything. All I was thinking about was getting short—going home. As you got shorter, it became worse. You might get killed and not make it home. You go into the jungle, it's peaceful and beautiful and quiet and strange. I hate the smell of gunpowder. It was scary, like fantasyland.

I went to Viet Nam with some *mayates.* I became good friends with them. They were good people. There was Henderson, Daygan, and Burdon, who got killed on that LP. These guys would hang out with other *mayates.* I was part of the gang, and we would fuck around together. Once we went to an EM club of another unit to drink beer. "Hey, what's that rabbit hanging around you for?" they told my *mayate* friends. "He's not a rabbit, he's my bro'," Henderson told the *mayate.*

After a while, they accept you but you don't feel comfortable because they called you a rabbit in the first place. "Fuck them, man," I told my friends, "let's get the fuck out of here, I feel uncomfortable here." I felt uncomfortable too, because I'm a Chicano, I'm not a *mayate*. I felt good with my *mayate* friends because we went to Viet Nam together. But when we got together with other people, I didn't feel good about that. I guess it's prejudice or something, but it's always there.

Another time some *mayates* got in a fight with these *gabachos* when they were walking back from the EM club one night. They got in a fight and the *mayates* kicked the shit out of this bad *gabacho*. Chicanos were neutral, but I was hanging around with my *mayate* friends. I was put in a spot, and I couldn't do anything about it because I was out of place. But, if it were Chicanos fighting *gabachos,* I would probably do something. I was in the midst of *mayates* and *gabachos*. If they would have been whipping my *mayate* friends, I would have helped them out. Most of these problems happened in secure areas. Sometimes back in the rear area we would think about fragging the CO because he used to volunteer us for dumb stuff.

The kids fell in love with us. They knew our names and stuff. But they liked the *mayates* better than the Chicanos. They went for the Black guys first, then the white guys second; the Chicanos were third. I guess they liked the black guys better because they knew how to talk and how to move. And the white guys because they were Americans. The Chicanos were Americans, too, but we were like gooks to them. We were far away from home and if you liked kids, you'd talk to them. They (kids) would give you weed or anything else they had. All they wanted was a couple of cans of C-rations.

There was a war going on, and the kids come to you and talk to you. They were beautiful people. They know a lot of things, more than my kid would. After a while, we would move out and never see those same kids again. The kids I knew wouldn't try to set you up to get killed, no way. I couldn't see

111

how some soldiers could ever kill those innocent kids. I couldn't do that.

The ARVN's used to go around the base camp holding and hugging each other. They used to wear tight fucking fatigues. I think a lot of them were fucking queers. A lot of the Kit Carson scouts would act like that, too. I got along with them okay, but they would come up to me and touch my butt. I'd say get the fuck out of here. Hey, I ain't going to fuck any fucking ARVN. I'd tell them to bring their sisters over instead.

We used to fight some North Vietnamese but more Viet Cong. I heard that the more GI's they killed, the easier they went to heaven. That's what the communist Buddhist believed. To the GI's, if you kill a gook you're still going to hell. The Vietnamese were fighting us because we were invaders. I believe that if someone invades your country, you should kill them. You can't get them out by talking because they are using violence.

The United States lost the war, and they would lose it again because there was no morale among the GI's. The gook is a small person but he's got a good head and there are a lot of them. They all look alike. Who cares if one dies. There's always somebody to take his place. Maybe ten guys would take his place because there were so many of them. I guess they had a better belief than our people because it worked for them. They kicked the big U.S. nation's powerful ass. They kicked them out of the land. That was because the United States couldn't use its big weapon—nuclear bombs. The gooks, one-on-one, kicked ass.

I was in a daze all of the time I was there. I couldn't believe I was there. I couldn't believe I was in a uniform and they gave me a rifle. They told me to do this and that. I couldn't believe my wife and son were far away. I was just doing it because they told me to. I was there because, to serve my time, I had to do it for a year. If I had to get up and do things and walk around, OK, I would walk around. But I wasn't going to kill nobody. If I get shot at, OK, I'll shoot back. That's all, *nomas.* That's the way I thought about it.

I got busted and I had to stay two more months over there. I thought I was going to go to LBJ (Long Binh Jail). They were telling me, "You fucked up, Delgado." My wife was writing to me and she was preparing for me to come home. And here I go and get busted. How could I tell her I got busted for four joints? I had to stand trial and I might go to prison. I was on my R&R leave and I had to go to the airport to get my plane. But I got involved with some people in a bar I was in. I met some ladies there and they invited me to their house. I was going to go to Sydney, Australia, for my R&R. I wanted to go over there because of all the *gabachas.* I got tired of that gook shit, no hair at all. I wanted beaucoup hair. I used to tell them, I want a mama-san with a big bush, big bush. "No big bush," they would answer.

I never made it to Australia. Instead I was going to stay with those women I met at the bar. I was going back to the base to pick up my bag, but I didn't know that there was a curfew. On the way back to the base, the air police noticed the Big Red One patch on my shoulder. I didn't know that we were restricted from that base. When they were searching and frisking me, they found four joints on me. They got me real hard, "What the fucks going on, guys? I'm on your side." The MP's were like bad *juras.* It was *gabachos* who beat me up. They probably thought I was Puerto Rican or something. After that they took me to some kind of jail in Saigon. They held me there until the MP's from my unit came to pick me up. I was still drunk when I woke up in the morning. I couldn't believe what was happening. I was supposed to go home in a couple of weeks. I started freaking out. I spent my R&R in jail.

I had to wait two months before my court-martial came around. Before this happened, I had everything planned. After I returned from my R&R, I would have only two weeks left in country. That meant I didn't have to go back to the field because they would pull you out of the field two weeks before your going home. Then I would have been living the life of a fat rat. Instead, I stayed in Viet Nam two more months than I was supposed to. All I did was pull bunker guard and odd ball stuff back at the base camp. It was the life of fat rat but I couldn't think that way. I couldn't trip like that because you know you might be going to jail. I was thinking they might fuck me over because I was Chicano, and I might lose the court-martial. I was thinking about going to LBJ and spending six or seven more months over there.

I was charged with possession of four sticks of marijuana or something like that. But I had a good record in the field, I was a good worker. All of my friends gave good character references at my court-martial. One of my character references lied. They asked him if he had ever seen Delgado loaded. He was a good E-5 sergeant, *gabacho* guy. He was a good guy, middle class and all of that. He said, "No, I never saw Delgado get loaded." He lied under oath. I owe him one.

My lawyer helped me out a lot. He found out that the police cut the paper from the four joints and put the grass on one side and the paper on another side. The lawyer got me off on a technicality. He told the court that the grass should have been left in the paper because how did he know that it wasn't tampered with. The court agreed and I was found innocent.

I couldn't believe I was going home. "I made it! I made it!" I thought, "I'm going home!"

RED DIRT AND RED DUST

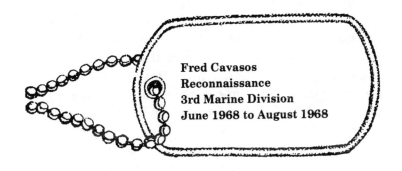

Fred Cavasos
Reconnaissance
3rd Marine Division
June 1968 to August 1968

I had been wanting to go into the Marines since I was fifteen years old.

When I graduated from high school, I was planning to attend Molar Barber College in Fresno. But after working all summer, I thought about my situation. I figured if I went to barber college I'd be able to finish it. Then I'd probably be drafted. So I decided it would be better for me to get the service over with first. So I enlisted in the Marines (instead of the Army) because the Army doesn't train you as well as the Marines.

When I got to Viet Nam, the red dirt and dust were the first things I noticed. It seemed like fertilizer or something. I also felt defenseless because I was not armed as we got off the plane. I felt like an idiot. I spent a week in training in Quang Tri along with the other Marines who had arrived on the same day as I did. We did some of the stupidest things I'd ever seen. For example, we'd go out at five o'clock in the morning on a three or four mile run in a tee shirt, shorts, and no weapons. The only one that was carrying a weapon was the instructor, and he was carrying a forty-five pistol. It was one of the dumbest things I'd ever seen. We would actually leave the compound unarmed. After this period of training we were sent to the Recon teams that we were assigned to.

The first patrol I went on was in the mountains of Khe Sanh. We worked real close to the DMZ. In fact, when I got hit, we were five to six miles from the DMZ. We used to get dropped by helicopter wherever they wanted us, and we would stay out in the field four or five days. Sometimes we did reconnaissance, seek and destroy, or we'd be on the side of the mountains and watch the valleys. If a movement could not be identified, it would be destroyed by air strikes or artillery.

At night we'd set up our claymore mines. We had two men on guard at all times, one manning the radio and the other standing up. This was very tiring considering we had four to six Marines on each team. We carried only food, water and ammunition. We never carried much of anything else— we carried between 125 to 150 pounds each. The first couple of patrols I was in, I took an M-79 grenade launcher, plus forty rounds of M-79 grenades, an M-16 and 21 magazines, plus a forty-five pistol, six hand grenades, 8 canteens of water and five days of food and a smoke grenade. During the short time I was there, I went on five patrols and was in two fire fights.

When we went on patrols, there were days when we wouldn't say nothing. Nobody would say a word. Sometimes I'd look around. I'd look at the guys and I'd think, "What are we doing here?" I knew we were fighting the communists and to keep communism from spreading, or something or the other. But I couldn't see how, if us five ran into five of them, and us killing each other, was going to change the outcome of this war. I still think about it now. How is it if I kill one guy it's going to change the war, but he's just as dead or I'm just as dead.

No, I couldn't see any sense in it. I used to think, man, we should be cruising, drinking, or something. I used to hear explosions sometimes from close off battles, or maybe from airstrikes. Then I'd think that's for real, people are actually dying. But it really didn't affect me very much because I think I was detached from it, I knew what I was there to do, but I didn't understand why. I remember seeing war movies and everybody is 35 or 40 years old. I mean we were 18, 19 or 20 years old, and some of the guys had been there a year. You grow up very fast. Fortunately, I never saw any of my friends killed or mutilated like some of the other Marines had. I thank God for that.

I didn't find out until later that we had been a target for two weeks. Two weeks prior to being artillered we had made a hit that caused a lot of damage. We were originally sent out on a sting-ray patrol, which is an ambush patrol. They sent another recon team to join us because forty Vietnamese had been spotted walking in the valley. So we and the other team, which made a total of nine men, were sent to ambush forty people. I thought it was stupid. When we got to the ambush site the Vietnamese never showed up. They were gone. So we split up into two teams and sectioned up some grid squares on the map to patrol. We started patrolling our section and came to a small hill. Below us was a river which we could see very clearly. In a short while we spotted two Vietnamese, so we watched them for awhile. It started to rain and they covered themselves with ponchos. We were pretty close to them, and we were trying to figure out if we should capture them or not. We called in to headquarters and told them we were going to continue to observe. Then, pretty soon, two more people showed up. Then two more guys and a woman showed up. We continued watching them, and then this one big guy shows up. They were all carrying little bundles and stuff. We waited about another half-hour and nobody else showed up. At this point, we decided to call artillery in on them. We were in such a position that if any of the rounds had fallen short, they would have hit us. After the artillery rounds hit, two cobra helicopters were sent in to attack. Then we opened up on them with our small arms, and then we went down to inspect.

They were all dead, except for one. He somehow got away. All we found was a cartridge belt held together by a small strand of belt. Apparently, he had gotten hit by some shrapnel which tore the belt. We found some tunnels leading from the river back to Dong Ha. We found out later that we had hit an NVA paymaster, and that wasn't so bad. The bad part was he was Chinese and we were able to prove that the Chinese were involved in the war. We grabbed the bundles and got out of there. We turned the bundles in and found out that they contained about 800,000 dollars worth of piasters.

From then on some strange things started happening every time we went on patrols. It seemed that every time we called in our coordinates, there were always some explosions a couple of hundred yards away. We thought it was coincidental at first. On the second day we called in and it happened again. We waited for about an hour before we called in some fake coordinates, and then there were three or more explosions. So, for three days no one knew where we were because we were calling in fake coordinates. We'd rather take a chance at being hit by friendly fire. On the third morning there was this barrage of artillery and one of the guys started laughing because that's where whoever was firing the artillery thought we were. We finally reported that there was something unusual going on.

It was not until the 3rd patrol that we eventually got hit. We had left LZ Charlie at about six in the evening. We traveled about three or four miles before we set up our night camp. Everything went fine that night. In the morning there were some strange events. Every morning we used to get up and move out by six, but this time we didn't. I guess the patrol leader felt safe because we were so close to the LZ. So instead of moving out and having breakfast at another location, we had breakfast there. About seven o'clock I was sitting down and resting, when all of a sudden there were some explosions about fifty yards away. The patrol leader said, "Find out where those are coming from."

I had the radio right next to me, and I started calling Kahn Tien. Before I got an answer all hell broke loose. Rounds were landing all around us, but none of us got hit. They just pitted the entire area around us. We had dirt, rocks and pieces of wood all over us. After the 155 mm rounds stopped, the patrol leader said, "Let's get out of here, just take your rifles and leave everything." I got up and as the patrol leader was calling on the radio, we heard some incoming and that one hit us.

It hit right where I was laying down. It is through the grace of God that I am still alive. The corpsman who was next to me started screaming. I didn't know I had been hit, but felt like a towel that had been popped. I remember thinking, "Man that was close." I had dirt all up in my eyes, mouth and under my nose. So I started cleaning all the stuff off. Then the patrol leader said, "I'm hit." He started calling names, four out of the six guys had been hit. When the patrol leader asked me if I was alright, I said, "Yea, I think so." By then I had gotten all the stuff off. I was still laying on my stomach. My pack was on my back, and I had grenades in it. I was lucky they were not detonated by the artillery. I started to get up and I couldn't. I turned around and there was nothing there. My legs were gone from the knees down. The knees looked like a big bunch of hamburger meat. I turned back around and I laid down and I said, "Yea, I'm hit." Then I just laid there.

I thought, "What should I do? Scream? Yell? It doesn't hurt." I was losing alot of blood, but it didn't hurt; I was just numb. I turned around again and by this time, the guys had gathered around. I saw the patrol leader get up limping towards me. He eventually lost one leg. By this time, Ski, the corpsman, had stopped crying and screaming. I was laying there on my stomach and I turned around again to see. The corpsman got my head and told me to lay back down because I'd go into shock. I was in physical shock but not in emotional shock.

119

The corpsman took an M-79 bandolier and applied a tourniquet around one of my legs. They found one of my boots with my foot still in it. The shoelace from this boot was used to apply a tourniquet around my other leg. I was laid out on a poncho and as soon as I was lifted, I went out. I wasn't out very long because I remember them carrying me and my hand was dangling from the side and bouncing on the dry grass. From then on, for the next fourty minutes, I'd wake up–pass out–wake up–pass out.

The corpsman's medical gear was blown up, and they couldn't give me any morphine. I remember hearing the helicopters, but they didn't want to come down because they were afraid of the artillery. A couple of guys called on the radio and they told them to get that so and so thing down or we'll shoot it down. There were four of us who were bleeding badly. Then some colonel got on the radio and said, "I'm colonel so and so," or something or the other, "and you shouldn't talk like that over the radio." They finally came down and as soon as I was put on the chopper, I went out.

I was taken to a tent in a medical unit. When I woke up, I was in terrible pain, I felt as if I was in the middle of a fire. They cleaned me up a little and then flew me to a hospital ship. I remember I was laying naked on the X-ray table. It was hard and cold. By this time I was yelling at them, "Put me out." They said, "Yeah, we'll do it as soon as we can."

I was unconscious for three days. First thing I saw when I woke up was a figure standing close to my bed. I caught a glimpse of this real shiny thing and I kept trying to focus on it until my eyes started to clear. When they did focus, the person also came into view. What I was focusing on was a cross. I thought, "Well, I've bought it." I thought the priest was giving me the last rites. He told me, "You know, don't you?" After a little while I knew I wasn't going to die. That priest helped me out a lot. My legs were left open for about two days after I woke up. My legs were patched up with bandages and benzedrine. They had to be changed every four hours. It was very painful because my legs were just raw bone and nerves at their ends. After they closed them up, the pain seemed to have been cut by seventy percent.

Being awake through the whole thing helped me a lot because I think it is a hundred times more devastating to a person if they are unconscious and find out that they lost their legs when they woke up. In a way it helped me, but in a way it did some damage because I set up a block. They told me about it in Japan. I wasn't reacting like everyone else. I was up and around in a wheelchair six days later. I wasn't laying around moaning and groaning. I saw no sense in it. Consequently, by the time I hit Japan they thought I was crazy. They sent a guy to talk to me because some of the doctors were worried about me. They thought that perhaps I was missing some marbles. During our talk he told me I wasn't crazy but that my mind had set a mental block and that it was going to melt someday—it took nine years.

Most of the nine years after I lost my legs I wasn't very concerned about who looked at me or what. But gradually I began to notice that when I went to a small store and if there were three or four cars parked outside, I would go to another store where there were fewer cars. Not because it was busy, but because there were fewer people there. Eventually it just messed me up for a while, to the point of almost committing suicide, and then I had a mental breakdown. You can shine it on all you want and pretend it's not there, or even have yourself convinced it's not there at all. But eventually it will catch up with you. I believe this is true for all Viet Nam veterans. It will catch up in one form or another. Interestingly enough, I found out a few years after I was wounded that our team, "Easy Flower," had been hit by ARVN artillery which had been infiltrated by the North Vietnamese because they wanted to get back at us for hitting their paymaster.

KOOL-AID AND
BIRTHDAY CAKE

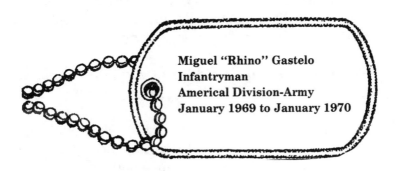

Miguel "Rhino" Gastelo
Infantryman
Americal Division-Army
January 1969 to January 1970

Where were your mother and father from?

My mother and father were from Hermosillo, Sonora, Mexico. In the 1920 s they moved to Delano, California and then our family moved to Corcoran in the early 1950 s. My father had to leave Mexico because he and his brothers had fought under Pancho Villa. He was forced to leave because of political reasons.

Where was your first permanent assignment?

I was sent to Germany at first, but I didn't like it there because there was too much harassment, so I volunteered to go to Viet Nam. Overall, I spent about five months in Germany. I got a thirty–day leave before I had to report to leave for Viet Nam. I also took 29 extra days on my own.

Soldados

Where did you arrive in Viet Nam?

Our plane landed in Cam Rahn Bay. It was very different
from what I had expected. Since I was infantry, I had expected
that perhaps we would start fighting after we landed. I got assigned to the American Division based at Chu Lai. I met some
people who were going home, and the infantry guys kind of
scared me because they were kind of loonie in the head, you
know, things like wearing sunglasses at night.

The first detail I was assigned to was the shit detail. I
thought they said that they were going to make me clean the
grease trap in the mess hall. But to my surprise, it really was a
shit detail: we burned shit mixed with diesel.

What unit were you assigned to within the American Division?

I was assigned to Company B 3rd Battalion 196th Light
Infantry Brigade, which worked out of LZ Center. When I first
got there, I thought this was going to be my home and that I'd
be going out on patrol everyday from here. But as soon as I got
there, I was put on a chopper that took me to my unit out in the
field. When we got to the landing point we began to draw fire,
and the chopper hovered about 6 feet off the ground. One of
the chopper gunners was firing his machine gun, and the other
one was kicking C-rations off the chopper, and he told me to
help him kick out all the boxes. So I helped him kick out all the
boxes, then he told me to jump. I said, "Wait a minute, why
don't you put the chopper down." He said, "No, jump," and I
said, "I can't jump," then he pushed me out. I fell down on the
ground, and the chopper just got up and took off. I didn't know
they were drawing fire because of all the noise the chopper
made and my inexperience. If I would have known we were
drawing fire, I would have jumped on my own.

After I landed, I looked around and there was nobody
around—just bushes and seven-foot jungle grass. I was sit-

ting there by myself with a whole bunch of C-ration boxes. As I saw the chopper fly away, I thought, "Goddamn, that's the last time I'll see that bird until I go home." As I was looking around I saw all these guys coming out of the bushes. These guys stunk bad and I was still clean with brand new fatigues on. They greeted and welcomed me. This one guy said, "What platoon you going to?" and then I said, "The Second." He said, "Oh, that's my platoon. Come on, I'll show you where we're at." He introduced himself, he was a Chicano from Sacramento. He took me to the command post where I met the Company Commander, he was a Mexican guy from L.A. From there, he took me to the platoon leader and then to my squad leader, he was also a Chicano. After all this, the rations began to be distributed. These guys were like animals. Every body wanted the same thing. Later on I found out everyone takes a turn in choosing—unless you got killed, then you never got your turn. Right away I saw a lot of cama-raderie. No one really fought.

What was a typical day like?

By daybreak we'd move out and go out about five miles or so, then we'd dig in and set up our day lodger. From there we'd go out on search and destroy missions. We'd cover about a five-mile radius. We'd get some sort of contact about three times a week. Then, in the later afternoon we'd move out to a night lodger, where we dug in again. Basically, this was what we did. Of course, sometimes we made very heavy contact which changed our routine.

Did you ever have any racial or ethnic problems with any of the troops?

Yeah, I remember a couple of times I had some problems. Once I got into a fight with a Puerto Rican back in the rear. It was a little unusual because back in the rear the Chicanos and

125

the Puerto Ricans would stick together. At times the Puerto Ricans had some hassels with the *negros,* and the Chicanos would back the Puerto Ricans. But I should make it clear that these types of problems usually occurred in the rear, in the bush everyone was much more together.

Anyway, after one of those stand-down shows, you know when everybody gets horney, bothered and pissed off, one of my Chicano *camaradas* invites me to drink over at the hootch of this one Puerto Rican dude who was a REMF. There were a lot of Puerto Ricans, about seven of them, and three Chicanos. And you know Puerto Ricans speak Spanish a little differently than Chicanos do. Well, there was this one Puerto Rican dude, who was drunk, who began to tell me that Chicanos didn't speak Spanish right, in other words, he was telling me that they were superior to us. That's when I told him he was sick from his *culo.* So the dude got mad and told me not to call him a REMF because he had also been a machine gunner. He knew I was a machine gunner because when my friend introduced us, he introduced me as a machine gunner. Then, he pulled out a small knife. He told me he was going to cut me and shit. I told him again that he was sick from his *culo.* At this point, the other guys began to calm things down. These guys were cool.

After everything settled down, I asked him to let me use his knife, and then I began to clean my fingernails with it. He got mad again and told me to give him back his knife. I was the son of a grand whore. I asked him if he wanted it back and he stuck out his hand, and that's when I stabbed him in the hand. He began to scream and cuss, "I'll kill you, son of a whore." The *vato* then began to come towards me, so I grabbed my M-16 and shot at the ceiling. I told him, "I'll kill your queer Puerto Rican ass." Then, this other Puerto Rican got mad because I started talking about Puerto Ricans. I was ready to shoot them motherfuckers. That's when my friend told me, "Fuck them, let's get the hell out of here." So we left. That's about the extent to where I got into a fight with the Puerto

Ricans. It was a little knife, but it did go through his hand.

Did you ever get into a hassle with the *gabachos*?

No, not really. But I did have a hassle with a *mayate*, though. It was in the summer time, and it gets to be a hot motherfucker and we were in a day lodger. Our platoon went out on patrol and we were the first ones back. What happened was that some cold Kool-Aid was brought in by chopper. There was this one *mayate* who was pissed because he had been transferred from the 101 airborne and he didn't want to be a grunt. Anyhow, he was one of the ones who was pouring out the Kool-Aid and there wasn't too much to go around. We all got our ration and he was telling us not to take too much Kool-Aid because we had to save some for the other guys. He was telling us this shit and he hadn't even gone out on patrol that day. After our platoon drank Kool-Aid, another platoon came in and drank some, and he didn't say shit to them. Then his platoon came in, they drank some, and he didn't tell them shit.

After his platoon stopped drinking he came back and filled up his canteen cup, and there was one platoon left to drink Kool-Aid. That's when I told him, "Hey, man, you're fucking around telling people not to get any Kool-Aid and what the fuck do you think you're doing." He said, "Motherfuck you, motherfucker." I opened up the lid of the container and told him to pour it back in. By this time everybody was gathering around. So I told him again, "Pour it back, motherfucker." He said, "Fuck you," then he took a drink out of the cup and threw the rest on the ground. By then he pissed me off man, and I had my M-16 with me, I felt like shooting the motherfucker. So I went after him to hit him with the butt of my M-16. As this was happening all the other G.I.'s held us back. He had his M-16 too; it's a good thing he didn't pull it out and shoot me. He said, "Let me go, I'm going to kill the motherfucker." I told them, "Let me go." By this time they had taken our M-16's away, and they let us fight. He gave me some good ones. He didn't kick my ass though, but I hit him some good ones too. After a while the others stopped us.

When the last platoon got there, they found out what had happened and they wanted to kick his ass too. Even the other *mayates* wanted to kick his ass. Nobody did what he did, because everything was shared equally. Especially with something like that, you come back from a patrol—and it's hotter than a motherfucker—and you've been drinking stagnant rice paddy water all day. If they had some cold Kool-Aid, you wanted some of it too. Anyhow, that dude wasn't worth a fuck to hump, and he was an asshole.

Do you think the *Raza* that was there was different in their attitude toward their role in the war, than other racial groups?

I'll tell you, the Puerto Ricans and the Chicanos, and even some of the Gabachos walked the point and took all the other hazardous positions. The *negros* hardly ever walked the point. Most of them were all right people, but when it came down to doing their part, they didn't want to. They didn't want to walk the point, carry the radio or carry the M-60 machine gun. I really don't know why this was so, but maybe it has something to do with the *negros* once being slaves to the white man: but this is the way I saw it. The Chicanos and Puerto Ricans, I'll tell you, they did mostly everything, all the point walking and carrying the M-60. Whenever we got into contact with the enemy, they were the first ones up front. The *gabachos* would go along, but they'd let the Chicanos and the Puerto Ricans go to the front and they'd follow. In my combat experience, I never saw a Chicano or Puerto Rican back off— never—not once.

What was your position within the platoon?

The first week they let me slide, but after that, I walked point for two months straight. I really didn't know the danger of it until I hit a booby-trap. When I hit that booby-trap, I didn't know I had hit it. When I hit it, the second guy heard the fuse pop and he said, "Booby-trap." He was about ten meters behind me and he dropped to the left while I jumped forward. The third guy ran forward and to the right. That's where the booby-trap was, and it killed him, it messed him up real bad. I really felt bad, after that I didn't feel like walking point. After awhile, I carried the M-60 machine gun instead. The basic function of the booby-trap, besides killing, was to give the enemy a warning that we were in the area. The next day they ambushed us.

Why did you volunteer to walk the point and carry the M-60?

The reason I did it was that I knew I had to do my part; if somebody else did it, I didn't see any reason why I couldn't do it. Some of the *vatos* didn't want to walk the point, that's okay, because if you're going to put someone who doesn't want to walk the point or doesn't know what he is doing, it can lead to a disaster.

What was the heaviest contact you were involved in?

The heaviest thing we got into was in August of 1969. What happened was that there was an NVA Division in our area. Initially, we were supposed to go in first but the jarheads said they wanted to go in first. So they did. They went in with a company, we were going to go in with a battalion, this was in Qui Son province. The jarheads went in and they got ambushed real bad. There were about 15 to 20 survivors. They called in for reinforcement, so Alpha Company of our battalion was sent in, and they got ambushed too. But they did manage to pull some bodies out. The main reason we tried to recover bodies was so we could send them home. The enemy didn't pull them back for that reason. The reason they pulled them back (dead bodies) was to fuck with your mind and to say they (U.S. Forces) didn't get nobody.

After Alpha Company was sent in and trapped, we were sent that same afternoon. As we walked in, our point man was shot and killed. When we reached Alpha Company, they were scattered all over the place. There were many wounded and dead laying all over the place. It began to stink badly, and at this point, we realized we were also trapped. We were trapped for about nine days. There were maggots all over the bodies as they deteriorated. This one dude got hit in the arm and the next day he had gangrene and maggots all over his arm. The smell began to get worse because of all the dead. I guess there must've been at least 100 dead bodies. We finally ran out of food and water about the fourth day. They dropped food for us, but most of it fell outside of our perimeter and the NVA got most of it.

During the time we were trapped, we were getting shot at all the time. We couldn't sleep with all that racket and harassment. The bodies sort of melted in the jungle, you couldn't even tell what race the bodies were, all you could see was the wet imprint that the bodies made on the ground. We couldn't eat in peace with the flies all over the place. They'd get on our food after eating on the dead bodies. The last two days we didn't receive any food at all; we began to eat weeds. We got so hungry that I remember one of the soldiers and me glancing at the side and seeing the open arm wound of one of the soldiers, and then him saying, "Man, that meat looks good."

Was there any effort to bring reinforcements to try to get you out?

Yeah, Charlie Company was ordered to go in, but they flatly refused. They all stuck together because they did not want the same thing that had happened to the other companies to happen to them. So, the next day Delta Company was sent to help us. They were smarter than we were and didn't try to go directly in like we did. They waited it out to try to figure out what was going on.

By this time the battalion commander, who had been flying around in a helicopter, found out what was going on. Actually, it was the first sergeant who figured it out because we heard them talking on the radio. Our command saw that there were two circle perimeters around us. One of the circles was keeping us in, while the other one, which was outside of the second one, was keeping people out. They were real smart because if any of the other companies really wanted to come in, they'd leave a hole open to let them in, and then they would be trapped too. I think they let it be known intentionally that they were there so we could fall into their trap. Command called this "Operation Birthday Cake" because the various perimeters formed made it seem like a cake.

That's when our battalion commander got shot down because they were flying too low. They got hit with an RPG right on the gas tank. It was the battalion commander, his RTO, the first sergeant, two chopper gunners, two pilots, and one AP and UPI reporter. they were all killed. When they got shot down they landed outside our perimeter and we had to go pick them up. By the time we found them, the gooks had already gotten to them. It took us about two days to find them, because we didn't know where they were and the enemy was after us too. When we found them, the colonel's *verga* had been cut off and put in his mouth. The first sergeant was buried up to his chest with one hand raised. The RTO was buried up to his neck, the chopper gunners, pilots and reporters were left alone. When we got them they were already turning gray, we could see their bones and their hair falling off, and they stunk bad. We put them in bags and took them back to our perimeter.

Prior to this operation, the battalion commander had

gotten our company together and told us he wanted a body count. He was handing out purple hearts and the *vato* said he was proud of the men that had received these medals and that maybe next time he could hand out some more. Then he said, "Men, we're doing a good job in this area. We're cleaning up the area of the enemy, but we need more body count. I don't care what it takes or at what expense." When he said that, I thought, "The motherfucking commander doesn't give a shit about us."

I remember a Puerto Rican medic who ran to help a guy who had gotten hit. Before he got there, he got shot seven times, once in the shoulder, in the stomach twice, twice in the leg and I don't remember where else, but he got hit bad. He was all fucked up and he still worked on the wounded guy. Those medics were good dudes.

How did you finally get out?

Well, after Battalion figured out what was going on, they placed a perimeter around the two perimeters the NVA had around us. And now the NVA were trapped, or so we thought. On the ninth day of our entrapment, the NVA created a disturbance on one end of the perimeter in order to attract the attention of our firepower. While some of their troops were doing this, the majority of them got out by tunnels leading outside of our outer perimeter. They did a number on us that time.

How did you feel when it was time to go home?

When it was my turn to go home, I had mixed feelings. I really wanted to go home, but I felt bad about leaving my *camaradas* behind. I left the field on the second of January, by the fourth I was in Fort Lewis, Washington, and by the fifth I was in San Francisco. It was raining real bad. From there I took the bus to San Jose, where my sister-in-law picked me up. The next day my brother Vincent took me to Hanford where my mother was living. It was strange. I was real glad to be home, but at the same time, I felt like going back to Viet Nam—why, I don't know.

As far as your experience in Viet Nam is concerned, and the present day political situation in Central America, what would your advice be to young Chicanos about the possibility of their going to fight in Central America?

My advice to an individual, a young man, would be to do what he feels is right. As far as the government being involved in other countries, I have no qualms with that. I'll back up the government anytime. I live in this country and I should abide by the country's rules. If they were to ask me to go to another war, I'd go, not that I wouldn't be scared, but I'd go.

How about sending one of your sons?

As far as sending one of my sons, I wouldn't ever really want to see one of them going to a war. If they had to go, or decided to go, I wouldn't stop them. It's one of those things where there is a lot of freedom in this country, and who's right or who's wrong, I don't really know, but the thing is that we live in this country and we should back the government. It's one of those things a young man has to think about whenever his turn comes up. As my personal experience goes, no one asked me to go to Viet Nam, I volunteered. It helped me grow up.

HUMAN BILLBOARDS

Diego "Blind" Garcia
Truck Driver
1st Logistical Command-Army
January 1969 to January 1970

I was drafted on April 26, 1968. I was working in San Jose, California, for Garden City Disposal Company at the time. My draft board was still in Kings County, so I had to report to Fresno for my induction. If they hadn't drafted me, I would have probably volunteered. I was thinking about volunteering for the Marines. Mike Soliz kept telling me that we should volunteer for the Marines, but I decided against it.

When I got inducted, I thought we were going to be sent to Fort Ord, California, for our basic training. Instead, we were sent to Fort Lewis, Washington. That part of the country is pretty, but it rains just about every day. When we got there in April, it was a trip because when we looked out the window it was snowing and we asked, "Hey! What's that white stuff on the ground?" When we left Fresno it was about 87 degrees. This was also the first time I had ever been on an airplane, so everything was a big trip.

It was an experience. When we got off the bus, there was a guy yelling at us, telling us, "You're mine now," and a whole lot of other bullshit. He was there kicking some dudes in the ass. He didn't kick me, but he kicked some other guys. He was a teeny-weeny, loud-mouth motherfucker. Those guys are perfect for that because the army shows you how powerful they are, by having such a little *vato* doing this to you. As they told us, "You can either make this a long two years or a short two years." In other words, play the game or get screwed.

From Fort Lewis I was sent to Fort Hachuca, Arizona, for vehicle driving school—truck driving. When I was there, they gave us a test and they told me, along with five other guys, that if we scored high in a certain test, they would send us to Fort Rucker, Alabama—some sort of chopper school. I didn't know what it was going to be because I didn't stick around long enough. I didn't like the idea of flying around. So what I did when I got to the school, I just went AWOL all of the time ... being late.

So, what they did was assign me as permanent party there in Fort Rucker in a quartermaster unit. I was there from August until early December. In early December I fell on a levy for Viet Nam. Our company was going to have a big inspection at the time. The commanders panicked and gave everybody who wasn't going to be assigned to the company permanently, or who had orders for Viet Nam, an immediate leave. We didn't even get paid. I had to go to Lemoore Naval Air Station to get paid.

When I was on leave, all I did was party. I was having a good time with my cousin Yogi. He had already been to Nam and he told me not to worry about it. I would watch the news on TV and see the guys in rice paddies ducking down. Two weeks later it was me ducking from those bullets. This happened when we were on convoys and we got hit. All of a sudden we were getting shot at and you hear the bullets just zinging past you. I could have gotten out of going to Viet Nam because I was the only son in the family. My sister was a beautician, and she knew some government officials who could have helped me get out of going to Viet Nam. I thought about it, but what the hell, I wasn't going to be the first only son that had gone to war.

By the third day, I was in Viet Nam; I was sent to Long Binh. I was assigned to a transportation unit, and right away I began driving trucks. Long Binh was on the outskirts of Saigon. We mostly hauled stuff back and forth from Long Binh to Newport Beach, which was about ten miles away. It was good duty because the Newport Highway was paved and it was in a free-flow zone. This meant it was very well guarded by armored personnel carriers, and it was heavily patrolled by the MP's. It was so well protected that we didn't even carry weapons.

That duty was okay, but about thirty days after I got there, I was sent on temporary duty to Tay Ninh, Chu Chi, Quon Loy, and Black Virgin Mountain. Black Virgin Mountain was just one big hill, a big gigantic hill, and on top of it was a radar station. Tay Ninh was about five or six miles away from there. Tay Ninh would get rocketed so much that it was called Rocket City. What we did in these areas was haul stuff out to personnel carriers, mostly fuel, oil, grease and air cleaners. We'd do that once a week. It would take us a day and a half to do that. On the way back we would often be under fire because they knew what we were doing.

To tell you the truth, I had it made over in Nam. Except for the time I was on TDY, I had access to all of the cold beer I wanted. All the steaks I wanted. All the fresh milk I could get my hands on, and milk was hard to get. I love milk and freshly made beans. We used to haul these refrigerated trailers. We would haul them off from Newport Beach where we would off load the ships. It wouldn't be nothing to rip off two or three boxes of steaks off them suckers. Our company area was the only one that had a freezer over there. We didn't go a day without eating a porterhouse steak. That was when I was in Long Binh. Boy! Did I suffer when they shipped me off to that temporary duty. *Me dieron en la madre.* It hurt my appetite deeply. The most precious thing down there in Viet Nam was ice. We had it. We were drinking cold beer and we'd be trading for air conditioning. Some of those dumb things never did work. We didn't give a shit anyway as long as we had it. The only thing we couldn't get was a television. I saw some sorry shit down there, but I couldn't bitch because I had it made. We worked long hours and afterwards we partied a lot. All we needed was two or three hours sleep to keep us going. We even drank when we were driving. We always had those green insulated canisters full of cold beer and sodas.

One time, I went seven days straight from Saigon to Tay Ninh hauling ammo to the Twenty-fifth Infantry Division. The first day I made the trip, the Vietnamese had just killed this gook. They strung that poor dude up on barb wire and they kept him up there for at least five days. They did that to put fear into the communists. He didn't look good the first day I saw him, so you can imagine how he looked the fourth and fifth day I saw him. They made a human billboard out of that guy.

I had seen another Vietnamese that was hung right outside of Lai Khe, which was the headquarters for the Big Red One. I had seen him the first day I made the trip and about three days later I was on a convoy when I noticed that he was still hanging. Two days later I asked a *camarada* of mine where he was going that day, and he told me that he was going to Lai Khe. I asked him to let me know if the dude that was killed was still hanging. When he came back that evening, he told me, "Yeah, man, that guy you told me about is still hanging, except that they turned him upside and he is hanging by his feet instead of by his neck."

We spent sixty days on TDY before they sent other drivers to replace us. When I got back to Long Binh was when my problems with the service began. There was too much harassment in Long Binh. There wasn't so much harassment on the LZ's. The officers were always assholes—back stabbers. Oh! they could brag and brag and brag. You could always tell the cherry officers because they would be the ones all dressed up in starched fatigues in the morning. It only took about four days for these guys to be broken in right. They would get up in the morning feeling bad and exhausted. They'd have to get up at four A.M. and they had gone to bed at midnight, and that wasn't because they were partying, that was because they were working. Here I was a nineteen year-old kid being told by another nineteen year-old kid what to do. So I would just tell them that, when they would tell me I was doing something wrong, to show me how to do it. That is when they would have to get down and work like we did. I must admit a few of them were good and knew their shit.

When I came back for TDY, they wanted me to be the CO's driver. They wanted me to be a shine boy. I didn't last at that position. By the end of the first day, I was fired. He wanted me to do all sorts of stuff to his jeep, salute the proper vehicles and bullshit like that. How is a fuck-up like myself going to do all that bullshit? I had an attitude problem.

We used to crawl under the fence of the compound to sneak out to the village at night. One of those times I was busted for sneaking in a whore. Another time I got busted for outright disobeying an order. I just flat out refused to do what they told me to do. So, they busted me from E-5 to E-4. It was no biggy. A month later I was an E-5 again, and a day later after that, I was busted again.

That's when they caught me and some *camaradas* sneaking in a whore. We would get the truck driver that would go on the laundry run to bring the prostitutes in and out of the compound. We used to pay him ten dollars. That was a lot of money back in 1969. Me and my *camaradas* used to do that all of the time. We'd make about twenty to thirty bucks apiece. I wanted to go back to Tay Ninh, but they wouldn't let me because I couldn't keep my nose clean. I used to get in hassles all of the time. I even had an MP dog chase me up a roof one time. After he chased me up the roof, the MP's put a flashlight on me and told me to get down. They chased us because we had gotten in a fight with the lifers. "Get down from there," they told me,"We've already got your buddies."

I went to deliver supplies to military installations in Saigon a lot of times. One of my friends that came down with malaria was sent to a hospital in the Cholon district of Saigon. There were always a lot of MP's in Saigon. Those guys ran all of the whore houses. When we went to see our friend, we got to party in Saigon for three days. When we got back to Long Binh, they busted the highest ranking guy that was with us because we stayed one day longer than we should have.

I had this *mayate* friend who used to go to Saigon whenever he had a chance. He used to go down there even if he didn't have a pass. He had a lot of clothes tailored over there. He must of had about ten suits tailored. He knew a lot of the local people. One day, one of the shoeshine boys told him to get out of the area. A little bit after he left, there was an explosion in that area.

I couldn't get along with the Vietnamese then, and I can't get along with them now. The only time I would talk to them was when I had to get laid. They would do it for a carton of Salem cigarettes.

You always had to watch out for the little kids because you didn't know what they were up to. It wasn't too bad in Saigon because I guess the people there understood that we were trying to do good. But out in the countryside, it was a different story. We had some guys blown up a few times when they let those kids get too close to them.

I couldn't get along with the Puerto Ricans because they were too cocky. I got in several fights with them. I had a *mayate* friend that used to call them imitation Chicanos and *mayates.* He used to call them that because he thought they were funny because he didn't think they knew whether to be black or brown. "Somebody fucked up when they made them," he would say. I had a problem with the Puerto Ricans. I'd call them *putos* and they'd call me *coño.*

I got along with the *gabachos* pretty good, but I got along with the *mayates* better. Man, me and some of those *vatos* used to party a lot, especially on them opium joints.

My *camarada*, Juan Guerra, used to fight Puerto Ricans all of the time. There wasn't a day that would go by that he would't get in some kind of argument with somebody. He was from San Antonio, Texas. He was a loud-mouth, you could hear him over anybody. If he couldn't handle the situation, his blade could. He was a skinny dude, he might've weighed about 130. He would want to fight right away. I guess it was a natural habit.

We were drinking in a bar in Newport Beach when he got into a hassle with some Puerto Ricans. I kept telling him, "Hey, we got to leave because the last truck is leaving for Long Binh, and we have to be back by reveille." But he didn't want to leave because he was pissed off with this one Puerto Rican. That Puerto Rican was a big dude and he was ready to kick Juan's ass. Juan just walked up to him and cut him. After that, we just took off in a hurry.

About two weeks later, we were at the PX in Long Binh and this one *vato* recognized us from the bar and turned us in to the MP's. We went through a court-martial. We spent about two days in jail before we went to the hearing. I got a lot of sleep there. When the hearing came up, the Puerto Ricans testified against us but they couldn't prove it was us because we were never reported AWOL. So they had to let us go: military justice.

Juan once tried to burn down the lifers' hootch. Another time he got his ass whipped by some *gabachos*. We were in a bar and he was so stubborn that he kept going back to the *gabachos* and they would kick his ass every time he went back. "Come on, Diego, we can do it. We can whip their asses." "Fuck no," I told him, "we can't do it." He didn't take his knife out because he was too loaded on beer. I finally grabbed him and we took off. I thought them white boys were going to whip on my ass too. After that, the MP's picked us up because we

Soldados

were staggering all over. They got us for drinking in public.
We resisted and they kicked our asses and put us in jail
again.

THE CIB

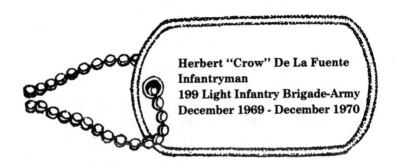

Herbert "Crow" De La Fuente
Infantryman
199 Light Infantry Brigade-Army
December 1969 - December 1970

Me and Manuel Gonzalez went to the induction center for our physical examination on the same day. Manuel told me that he had gone to a *curandera,* and that she was going to help him in not passing the physical. I passed the physical and he didn't.

After my basic and advanced infantry training at Fort Ord, California, I found myself in Viet Nam. When I got there, I was assigned to a recon platoon. As soon as I was out in the bush, they told me they needed a new pointman. This guy named Black broke me in. He was a real *loco* from Oklahoma. He always had a dead Vietnamese's ear hanging from his hat. I first met him back in the rear. He was there because he had gotten the clap, and he needed to be treated. He broke me in within a week.

After a while, I liked walking the point because I knew what I was doing and I didn't have to be accountable to anybody. Walking the point meant that I knew what was going

143

on in front of me. Walking in the middle or rear of the file made it difficult to know what was going on in front of you. One of the first times that we received contact I was walking in the middle of the file and I heard firing in front of me. A little afterwards I heard a shot behind me. This guy had shot one of our guys in the leg accidentally. These things can happen if you don't know exactly what is coming down.

One of the times that I was walking point, we were looking for some enemy mortars that were firing at our base camp. We got to a place at the bottom of a hill, and I figured that they had to be at the bottom of the hill. At this point we took a break. I told Black, "You know what? Man, there are some old trails that already are covered with bamboo. Should I cut it or go around it?" He told me I should go around it. But then, the lieutenant came around and told me to cut the bamboo.

I did what he told me, but I was going real slow in cutting the bamboo. Then the *vato* called me back and told me I should cut a little bit faster. I told him I wasn't going to go any faster. That's when he told me to walk the rear. "Hell with it," I told him, "I'll walk the rear." But I didn't go all the way to the rear, instead I got behind the RTO.

They sent up another pointman to take my place. The guy went to the same spot that I was at and they (enemy) opened up the clamors on him. The clamors, for some reason, were facing the opposite way and nobody got hurt. The first chance I got, I really chewed that lieutenant out. Later on that day, we got a couple of the enemy by ambushing them. We caught them half-stepping as they were bopping down the trail.

Another time we had the opportunity to overrun a Vietnamese base camp. That was one of the most exciting experiences I had in Viet Nam. That day Black was walking point when we came to the bottom of a hill, and Black and our scout figured that the enemy was at the top of the hill. Black didn't think that there were that many and that we could take them. And sure enough, we did. We crossed the river to climb the hill. We went up the hill and overran the camp. We didn't find any bodies, but we found a lot of flags.

We would usually go out for about two weeks at a time. We had firebase Teresa where we would take showers and clean up and get our mail. After a couple of days of that, they would fly us out again to begin another operation.

On one of those operations, we were on a well-used trail. It must have been some time around the Tet season. I was standing guard on the trail so that the other soldiers could cross it. That's when I saw this little bastard coming down the trail. That fucker looked at me, and I looked at him. I raised my rifle and shot three rounds at him before it jammed. I'm not sure, but I think I managed to hit him. I called Black and told him I saw a gook. Me and Black went up to where I shot that bastard and all we found were his sandals.

We went up a little ways and we found a bunker. So, we dropped a couple of grenades into it, but there wasn't anything in there. We went up a little ways more and we did the same thing to another bunker we found. Then, all of a sudden we heard those fuckers yakking. There were only three of us up there so we decided to go back down the trail. We called for one of those Loch helicopters to come and pick us up at the bottom of the hill. When the chopper got there, the pilot told us, "Hey, you guys better get the fuck out of here because there's a couple of battalions of Viet Cong up there."

The next day, after the cav had skirmished with the enemy, we went up in a helicopter to see what had been up there. As we got close to the site, we saw a blown up tank and all kinds of other stuff all torn up. We were lucky we hadn't gone up any higher than the previous day because that would have been it for us.

About the sixth month of my tour, I had developed a pretty bad nervous problem. What happened was that my hair began to fall off. As soon as I had gotten back from my R&R, we were to go into Cambodia the next day. I didn't want to go. We were airborne when the order came down for us to return. I said, "All right." I was happy like a big dog. As soon as we got back, I went to go see the medics. I told the doctor I couldn't take it no more. He asked me what was wrong and I told him I thought that the stress was getting to me. He gave me an examination, and a couple of days later he gave me my papers that called for me to get a rear job.

I went from Bien Hoa to Da Nang which was north of Bien Hoa. I thought that since I was going up north it was going to be worse. But, it wasn't. I had a real good assignment with a security unit. I really enjoyed my last six months in Vietnam. We used to patrol the port and city of Da Nang. Compared to being out in the bush, this was heaven.

We shared the compound with an engineering and medical unit. The engineering unit was almost all Mexican, the majority of them were from Texas. We had taken over the compound from the Navy. The conditions were real good, we had air-conditioned barracks. You talk about partying out, man, we really did. We'd get on a jeep and go out to Da Nang and pick up some hookers. We'd bring them into the compound and tell the guys, "OK, boys, bring out your money." We used to confiscate *grifa* from the Vietnamese and sell it in the barracks.

All of the PX shipments would come into Da Nang port. We had a lot of Koreans who would unload the boats. I got in pretty tight with them. A couple of times, I asked them to drop a couple of pallets that had all kinds of stereos and TV's. The pallet would fall and break. In my hootch I had a TV, stereo, stove and a refrigerator.

When I went on patrol at the port, I'd take a couple of cases of C-rations to give to the gooks. I don't know why I called the Vietnamese gooks. I guess because everybody did. And when I needed something, they would help me out. If you treat people good, they treat you good back. The Vietnamese people treated me good.

I was thinking about making the Army a career for a while. I wanted to be a drill sergeant. After coming back from Viet

Nam, my attitude changed. I stayed AWOL for two months before I was supposed to report to Texas. When I reported to Texas, they busted me from E-4 to E-3, and I was in a restricted company for sixty days. I didn't really care because even though I got busted, they couldn't take my CIB away.

I did my time by being restricted to the company area and doing extra duty *y la chingada.* One day the Lieutenant asked me if I wanted a three-day pass. I hadn't any days off since I had been restricted, so right away I accepted the offer.

They gave me the three-day pass, and I went back to Fresno. I stayed AWOL for another month. By then, I didn't care anymore. But, I went back and did my time.

THE POW

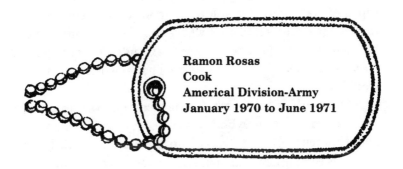

Ramon Rosas
Cook
Americal Division-Army
January 1970 to June 1971

I n my unit everybody was on some sort of drug—barbiturates, marijuana, heroin, opium, speed or alcohol;
our mess sergeant was an alcoholic. They worked us cooks
real hard, and it was real hot in those makeshift kitchens.
After work, there really wasn't much to do. Once a week, they'd
show some movies, but that's about all the entertainment we
had. In our spare time we'd usually go to the bunker where our
friends were pulling guard. Everyone pulled guard, so we
knew everybody that was pulling it. That's where the party
was at. After we partied, I'd go to my hootch, and sleep. I'd get
up and smoke a joint, and then I'd go and feed the soldiers:
after awhile I got hooked on barbiturates (BT's). I always had
a case of hand grenades and C-rations under my bed, just in
case I got hungry, or we were attacked.

The first night I was there one of the POW's escaped.
Supposedly, this high officer in the North Vietnamese army
was on the loose and they didn't know where he was. Nobody

knew if he'd gotten out or not. At about five in the morning he tried to jam outside the perimeter and they got him with an M-79 grenade launcher. They hit him real bad, half of his body was blown off. Everybody was walking up and checking out the body. As I got close to where his body was, I stopped dead in my tracks. Heck, I didn't want to see no more, man. I just made a U turn and went back to my bed. I just wanted to go home right there and then. I thought to myself, "What am I doing here? Does this go on everyday?" When I learned the ropes, some of the other soldiers and me used to sneak out to the village at the same spot where that Jap-Vietnamese got hit. After I was there for a year, I extended for another six months of my Viet Nam tour. That's when I got into trouble.

My troubles began when a new captain was brought in and started giving everybody a hassle. He came in talking shit about haircuts, clean fatigues and bullshit like that. Everybody was coming down on him, and he was a Black guy at that. The *mayates* didn't like him. They were talking about fragging him, *y quien sabe que.* During this time I was strung out on BT's real bad. So one night I was all messed up on BT's and I was passing by the captain's hootch where he was sleeping. I had that case of grenades handy under my bed so I just went over and got one and came back to his hootch and threw it in. I fucked him up—I regret doing that, but I was just fucked up at the time. As it happened, he heard the grenade fall and he pulled up his mattress to protect himself. But, his leg was sticking out, that's where it got him. It didn't blow his leg off, he recovered pretty good because he was there at my court-martial.

Immediately after this happened, they went directly to two Black guys who were always talking about getting the captain. They put them in jail for a month before they even knew I had done it. I guess they snitched on me after they found that they were going to be convicted of the fragging. That's when they came and got me. I told them and my lawyer that I had done it. By this time it had been working on my mind. I was all fucking down. By then I was really eating those BT's. They even took my weapon away from me.

My lawyer helped me out a lot. I guess he investigated my background and saw that I had never done anything like that. In fact he told me that I deserved three years in prison for what I had done. He told me that if I considered it again, I probably wouldn't do it again. And that it was probably the monotony that made me do it. The lawyer told me we would plead innocent and we would go from there.

Before my court-martial I spent some time in jail at the Da Nang stockade. By the time I got to jail my Black friends had been there and gone already. In fact when they were taking me to jail, these two captains and some MP's had to stop by this bunker and arrest this *mayate*. What had happened was that all these *mayates* took over a bunker and they wouldn't let nobody near. They had kicked all the white guys out. I mean, man, these guys were shooting the officers and NCO's that would be passing by and stuff like that. They arrested this one guy because supposedly he was the one who had done the shooting. Heck, they didn't know exactly who had done it. They just picked on this particular guy. These Black guys were hooked on heroin. Some of them had been introduced to it back in the world. Shoot, when they got to Viet Nam the heroin was practically free, compared to back in the world. All them Blacks used to tell me, "Hell, I got my purple heart back on the street."

When I got to the Da Nang stockade they had maximum, medium, and minimum security. I was put in medium security at first. I worked real hard and then I was put in minimum security. This meant I could work outside the compound. I was there about three weeks when I had a problem with a guard. He told a bunch of us to do some work and nobody was doing it. He picked me out as if I was the leader of the people that told them not to work. So then, he told his superiors that I was the one that was telling them not to work. Heck, you didn't have to tell people not to work, because nobody wanted to work anyway, we were in jail. As a result of this, I was sent back to medium security. I told my lawyer about what had happened and he told me he couldn't do anything about it.

After about a month or so, I finally had my court-martial. The key witnesses were those two *mayates* who at first had been charged with fragging the captain. When their turn came up to testify, they were so fucked up on heroin that they couldn't even speak right. That judge looked at them, and then he looked at me, I guess he had pity for me or something. I was found innocent. I mean, these guys were so gone they could have arrested them for being under the influence. When we walked out of the courtroom there were all kinds of cameras. I guess it even came out in the Stars and Stripes newspaper. The lawyer told me, "Come here, let's take a picture together," and all the cameras took pictures of us shaking hands.

When I went back to my company it was completely different. We had a new company commander and he told me I could start a new life in the company. By this time I had about two weeks to go in country, so I tell the CO, "Does this mean I can extend for another six months." The CO got excited and said, "No, no, I don't think we can do that."

MUTINY

Charley "Fat Rat" Trujillo
Infantryman
Americal Division-Army
January 1970 to July 1970

We had been humping the bush for about three weeks when we were choppered out. As usual, we were not told exactly what we were up to. I dreaded those chopper rides, especially on those slicks because they seemed too vulnerable. It was worse than riding a carnival ride without any safety precautions. They would carry about four or five fully equipped GI's. And if you were on the end, your feet would dangle from the side. They would tell us not to worry because centrifugal force would keep us in, I still have my doubts.

After landing we were met by a company of tracks and we traveled all day with them. For us it was real nice because we at least did not have to walk. But, we were always alert. That evening we joined up with another company of tracks and the rest of our company. This was different for most of the guys in our platoon because we, for the most part, were used to fighting a guerrilla war in the mountains. We were not accustomed to being on flat land, or around as much noise as the

153

tracks made. Silence was a rule stricktly adhered to in the bush.

That night the tanks and APCs formed the basis of our perimeter, which reminded me of wagon train westerns. In the morning we ate our breakfast of C-rats, which were also our lunch and dinner. After eating we moved out and searched the surrounding foothills. About ten in the morning we received some mortarfire from the North Vietnamese. A few of the guys were wounded but there weren't any fatalities. I remember Bones, the Medic, calling out that he was hit. I ran to him and found him laying between a triangle of fallen mortars. He later told me I had scared the shit out of him by the astonished look I gave him. I thought he should have been severely hurt because of the nearness of the mortars that had fallen. Within a week he was back with us.

Throughout the day we received mortar and sniper fire. By that evening we had suffered more casualties. The one I remember most was a guy we called the yippie. He was totally against the war and usually tried to avoid any violence. He was even thinking, for a while, of not carrying a rifle. It didn't help him much because the dude lost his leg that afternoon. That evening we did the wagon train trip again. There were incoming mortars throughout the night and by morning there were more fatalities and wounded.

At first light, our company was sent to search the surrounding area. Our squad spotted a North Vietnamese soldier about 100 yards ahead of us going into a hole. We found the hole and threw grenade after grenade in there trying to get him. None of us would go in after him, though. In a way it seemed like hunting a jack rabbit. After a while we decided that he must have gotten out by another exit.

By mid-day we regrouped with some tanks and ate lunch. Martinelli, a soldier from Massachusetts who always seemed melancholy, traded some C-rats with me. As we ate he began to sing the song, "And When I Die," by Blood, Sweat and Tears. After eating we moved out in line, something else we generally didn't do. Before I knew it, I was in a trench and told to move forward. Jones, an M-60 machine gunner, was next to me when he began arguing with the company commander. Jones said he wasn't going any further and the CO threatened to shoot him. We moved out about thirty yards when people started falling from machine gun fire. Van Hetsman, who was to my left, was shot in the midsection. Fat Ronnie and I tried to keep him alive by giving him mouth to mouth resuscitation. Now I know why they teach in combat first aid not to tell wounded guys that they are going to be all right. They won't believe you. Fat Ronnie told Van Hetsman, "You're going to be all right." Van Hetsman gave him a look as if to say, "Sure, fucker." He died as we were giving him mouth to mouth; that's what they called, "kissing the dead."

I didn't know what was ahead of Fat Ronnie and me because there were some bushes right in front of us. All I could hear was the sound of machine guns and "Medic." After Fat Ronnie and I realized Van Hetsman was dead, we moved forward. We didn't do it wholeheartedly, but we had a moral obligation. To my surprise, all the commotion was taking place about eight yards from where Van Hetsman had been shot. In these situations, I found that reality seems surrealistic. Time, space, and perception were no longer what they used to be, or pretended to be.

Jones was shot through the neck, and Martinelli was shot in the chest with a dead black Medic on him. It is ironic that he died as the black Medic was giving him mouth to mouth because Martinelli hated blacks. He used to say, "I hate niggers," and here he died with a "nigger" giving him mouth to mouth. The Medic was shot, as were the other casualties, at almost point blank. The bullets of the AK went clean through his steel pot very neatly without making a mess. The CO and our platoon leader were both seriously wounded.

All in all, there were about 15 casualties. All this was done by four North Vietnamese. They had been dug in right in front of us. A helicopter had thrown red smoke on their

position. Jones and some of the others had seen the smoke
and that's why he told the CO he wasn't going in. But the CO,
out of his glory-seeking mentality, ordered a direct assault
which led to more wounded and deaths than there should
have been. He was such an idiot that he even wanted one of
the guys to stab one of the dead Vietnamese with his bayonet
in order to declare that he had stabbed him.

In the wake of this, I ran up and began shooting at the
dead Vietnamese in the holes, just as I had seen in the
Hollywood movies. As I did this, some captain on a track
started giving me some bull. I was feeling pretty strange and
he didn't know how close he came to getting shot. One of the
dead Vietnamese had his body buried upside down in a hole
with one of his legs sticking up. I tried to pull him by his leg to
see if he had any money and the leg started to come off, so I
stopped pulling on it. Then someone threw a face at me.
That's how bad some of the North Vietnamese had been
blown up by the grenades.

As we evacuated the wounded, it began to rain lightly.
What really upset me was that we stacked Jones, Van
Hetsman, Martinelli and the Medic up on one another. We put
them on the chopper as if they were sides of beef. They
weren't even put in body bags. As the helicopter took off, it
was eerie to see them with their eyes staring blankly toward
the sky and their hair blowing freely. They seemed to know
that they were dead.

As soon as the chopper had taken off, we began to receive
sniper fire. Ivie, one of the dumbest guys in the platoon, was
lying next to me. I began to snicker as I saw the seat of his
pants turning brown. At this point some of the soldiers
dropped their rifles and began to run toward the rear. I can't
say I blame them for running, but they shouldn't have dropped
their weapons. Shortly after this, we were ordered to pull
back. We were harassed all the way back to the village we had
used to regroup. Those North Vietnamese didn't know when
to quit. On the way back I was walking behind a tank when I

decided to climb on it in order to get some water. As I got on it, an RPG hit on the side and I was thrown off. I landed in a rice paddy and was stunned for a few seconds. I reached to see if my legs, arms and the family jewels were still with me. When I found that they were, I ran from the burning tank.

We finally arrived at the edge of the village. We looked like those guys in the Sergeant Rock comic books, tattered and exhausted. As we walked into the village, the South Vietnamese popular forces were playing volleyball. I began to think and try to make some sense out of what was going on. The South Vietnamese were supposed to be on our side and helping to fight the Viet Cong and North Vietnamese, but instead they were playing volleyball. The North Vietnamese, on the other hand, were very fierce and were kicking our asses. Something was not right.

Things were really getting to me. I was feeling very angry, especially toward the officers. When we got back I had an encounter with this guy named Riley. He had been a highway patrolman back in the world. I asked him where he had been when Jones and they had gotten killed. He told me that he had gotten heat prostration. I thought he was faking it. "Hell," I told him, "Don't you think the sun shines on me." Some of the *gringo* soldiers would at times get angry at me because they thought I was gung ho. I didn't feel I was gung ho, I just felt that I had to do my best. Just because I felt that way did not mean I should be cannon fodder.

Greenwood and a couple of the other Black soldiers who had thrown their weapons and ran, were choppered to an LZ where they met with the batallion commander. They didn't get into any trouble for running. Or to use the cliche, "Advancing in the opposite direction." Some of the black soldiers were saying things like, "The war's at home." This made me think for awhile. Actually, it was Greenwood who ignited the mutiny.

We were told that we were going in again in the morning. I, along with some of the other soldiers, told them that we refused to go in again. There wasn't any sense in it. It was clear by that evening that the majority of the soldiers did not want to go back in. A new company commander was brought in. He seemed like a sincere man and gave us a real good pep talk, just like those charismatic football coaches do. However, that didn't convince me or many of the other soldiers. We argued among ourselves through the night, the majority being against going in. The more we argued the more I was convinced it was stupid to go back in. We didn't receive any sniper or mortars throughout the night. But, in the morning a few individuals moved out on line towards the enemy as they were told. When these individuals moved out, the rest of us were more or less morally obligated to move with them. I did not move out with the first soldiers. I had told them that I wasn't going to. One of the first ones to get shot was the new CO. He died in the Medivac helicopter. There were some other deaths and one guy was even left behind. I'm glad I didn't know him. It seems as though the North Vietnamese had known what was going on and knew what they had to do in order to stop us. Within a few hours our company was picked up by helicopter and sent out to the bush where we continued our guerrilla war.

And I kept walking the point until I was also wounded and medivaced.

GOOD TIMES - BAD TIMES

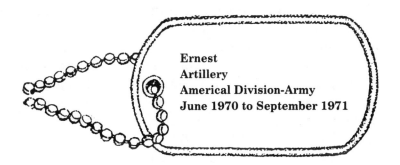

Ernest
Artillery
Americal Division-Army
June 1970 to September 1971

Most of the time I was in Viet Nam, I was in either LZ Snoopy or LZ Stenson. I went through three captains. The first captain I didn't know too well because he was only there for a month before his time was up. The second guy was a real prick. He tried to burn one of my buddies because he (buddy) called in some wrong coordinates on a village and the village was blown up. The third captain was only twenty-four years old. He came in kind of gung ho, but our first sergeant had done three tours in Nam. The sergeant told him, "These guys will help you if you help them." The captain took his advice and everything worked out fine. A short time later the first sergeant was sent back to the world because he broke his leg as he was going into the hootch of one of the hookers we had on the hill.

Our battery was the black sheep of all the batteries. We could outshoot everybody. Our guns were the best. We had junks but had them going. When something came up, something dirty, we had to go. We made a jump one day to some ridiculous outpost. They sent us in with two guns of ARVN's and two of our guns. They sent us up to a cemetery. We were building hootches on a cemetery. When we were digging, sometimes we would hit a grave and we'd just cover it up a little bit, put a mat on top of it and lay down. That used to piss us off because we were living like pigs. The ARVN's were always decked out in clean clothes and they also had the best equipment.

I used to have it in for the Vietnamese, but not anymore. I used to hate the ARVN's the most because we were supposed to be helping them and they were taking advantage of us. Now I realize that they were just trying to make a living like anybody else. The ARVN's were making bucks off the Americans left and right, pimping, selling drugs or anything else they could. One ARVN major who had *chieu boid* caught one of his men selling dope to the GI's on LZ Stenson. The major went up to him and shot him in the head, and the major just kept on walking. We gave the South Vietnamese a lot of support: food, equipment, arms, built houses and roads for them. Heck, Bien Hoa had better roads than Corcoran.

The ARVN's used to keep us up all night firing artillery rounds at shit that didn't mean nothing. Even the infantry guys who came out of the field would tell us, "Why are you guys shooting out there for? There is nothing out there." We wouldn't just shoot one or two rounds, we'd shoot 500 or 600 rounds. Once during monsoon, we shot for three straight days and nights. We stayed awake by taking obisital-liquid speed. It tastes like vanilla. The idiot who gave it to me didn't tell me you were only supposed to take just half a teaspoon. I took half and my buddy took the other half of the speed. We stayed up for three days firing. That is about the only time I really enjoyed shooting all night because we were helping the infantry from getting their asses kicked. It would make me mad when the dinks would call in useless targets.

We had kids on our hill who used to do our laundry. They

wouldn't let the ARVN's or the people from the village try and screw us. We had Vietnamese cooks and KP's who were pretty good people. There were whores all over, so we really didn't have to mess with the civilians. I used to feel sorry for the kids. We'd come down the hill with our trash of spoiled milk and slop on a 5 ton truck loaded to the top. Here you are driving the truck and you have kids, who can barely walk, try to jump on your truck to eat trash. Sometimes, you'd get pissed off because they would be throwing the trash out and you've got to go back to pick it up or pay them to put it back on the truck. By the time you'd get to the pit, everything was gone, and you have people eating up the slop on back of the truck.

You would feel sorry for the people. I remember I backed up into the pit one time and I was pissed off. I pushed one of the kids off the truck and he fell into the pit. It'd fill up with rainwater and trash. It was about twenty feet deep. When the kid fell in, I had to go in after him. I came out smelling like shit. What hurt me the most was seeing those kids starve. What got me one time was when we were shooting white phosphorous rounds and they brought in a kid who had gotten hit by the rounds. He was burnt bad, his face was half fried, and he was still alive.

Our battalion had the only swimming pool in Chu Lai and they wouldn't let us use it. Only the officers, nurses and shitheads could use it. One of the nephews of a famous jockey made sergeant by being a lifeguard. He made it by watching people swim—sitting on his ass. Can you imagine that shit? That's what really turned you against the army with the chicken shit way they treated you. There was no morale. The morale was a group of GI's sticking out for each other. They didn't give a shit about the army or the war. I lived in a small hootch, 12 feet by 12 feet, with twelve other guys. You got to know everybody's family and personal lives.

Back then was when they had the Black Power movement going on. By that time a lot of the colored guys started going over there with a chip on their shoulders. One day a

couple of black guys told me as I looked at them, "What the
fuck are you looking at, you mother?" My Black friend told
them, "Hey, that's my partner." "Fuck that dude," he said. I
just turned around and told them, "Hey, go fuck yourselves."
I carried a switch blade, so I wasn't worried. One of the guys
wanted some shit and he came towards me. I grabbed a dud
grenade and pulled the pin and told him to come and get it.
"Naw, man," he said, "the guy is cool, the guy's cool." I was the
only Mexican on the hill, and I got along good with both Blacks
and whites. Sometimes the Blacks would complain about
the whites and the whites would complain about the Blacks. I'd
tell them, "What can I say, I'd rather stay out of it. I ain't got no
shit with either of you races. What's going on here is that I am
trying to get my ass home." The morale was pretty bad there
for a while. Everybody was at everybody's throats. It mel-
lowed out after a while.

We used to go to Qui Ny City once a week. They had a
MACV compound there that had an air conditioned bar. I
once sat in that bar between an Arab and a Jew. I sat there
between them and listened to them argue. At that time, I
didn't know what the hell was going on between Arabs and
Jews. Those suckers sat there all afternoon drinking boiler
makers. They left as friends. As soon as I walked out, I passed
out.

We had some good times and bad times. I had seen some
of my buddies flip out with personal problems; mostly dear
Johns and divorces. I saw one guy flip out completely. He kept
seeing gooks, so we let him fire all night long. We just carried
the ammo to him. The Viet Nam War was a waste of good lives
and time, half the people didn't know why they were there.
They say to fight communism, but shit, the South Vietnamese
didn't want to fight, while we were busting our asses and
losing people left and right. After a while I started questioning
what we were doing there. Why are we spending all this
money? Money ain't shit when it comes to lives.

We had a fire-mission one night and I was hauling ammo.

Our hootches were underneath the ground, with about four feet of hootch above the ground. That night the guys turned the guns on me when I was asleep. As I was sleeping they told me, "Hey, get out." As I came out of the hootch, the guns went off. They had very high explosives charge motherfucker-charge seven. I'm not kidding you, the concussion from the guns picked me up in the air, flipped me up and knocked my drawers off. I was completely deaf for a month. They sent me to a battalion hospital. I didn't have to do anything but eat and sleep. I'd wake up at eight and didn't have to make formation. My ear drums were both torn. They were ready to ship me out to Japan when my ears healed.

For my R&R, I went to Hawaii. My fiancee was supposed to meet me there, but she never made it. I then decided to go to San Jose, California, and see what was going on. I went to a shopping center in Honolulu and bought me some civilian clothes. After that, I took a airplane to California. It didn't work out. Maybe it's for the better, I don't hold any grudges or anything like that.

Half of the guys on the hill were lushes and the other half smoked pot. Then you had your hardcore, about five per cent, who were heroin addicts. The addicts were no problem as long as they did their job and kept out of the way. I had seen one guy take all the guts out of a radio and with candle wax, seal all kinds of vials filled with heroin and cocaine. He went to Hawaii. When he came back, he was still talking to his wife. He made some bucks because his wife took a lot of the stuff back home.

Many times, we didn't get enough to eat, so we'd go to the battalion supply room. One guy would bullshit whoever was taking care of the supply room. I'm not ashamed to say it, but we'd go in there and steal the food. We'd also raid the supply room when we were pulling guard and smoking dope.

One night we got hit. And you always got one guy that's a mama's boy. This guy panicked and froze. He wouldn't fire the sixty machine gun, so I went into the bunker and hit him. I

163

took the machine gun from his hand and began to fire it. I always pulled the machine gun to the side of the bunker because that's the first thing they are going to hit.

I ran over and killed a dog while I was on the mail run. Someone got mad and shot at my truck. I ducked down and hauled ass. I think I ran over somebody's dinner. Another time, I was going after the mail one morning and I saw this guy taking a piss off a track. I said to myself, "I know this sucker." It was Fidel Trejo. I had also seen Joe Navarro and Bosco over there. Dickie Holguin was there and so was Pete Holguin and Billy Jordan. But I never got to see any of those guys from Corcoran.

I was scheduled to go to Fort Carson, Colorado, after my tour in Nam. When some of the guys told me how bad it was in Fort Carson, I extended my tour in Nam for another six months, so when I left Nam I would be out of the army.

I had about two weeks left in country when we flipped a coin to see who was going to Khe Sanh. It turned out that I didn't have to go. The truck that I would have been driving was hit once on the way down there, and it was blown up about a week later. I found out about this later on from one of my buddies from Lemoore. He said they got their asses kicked every day for a week. They'd chase charlie up to the DMZ, and they'd be chased back at night. Half of our gun unit was killed. Half of the gun unit (6 men) were juicers and the other half were pot heads. What happened was that the juicers stayed at the gun site to drink and the potheads went over to another place to smoke pot. The juicers got hit by a direct mortar round and they got snuffed. That guy from Lemoore came home pretty burned out, too. "Pot saved my life," he told me.

Another good friend of mine from Sonora, California, got all strung out on drugs. I went to visit him a couple of times. He was a pretty tight dude. About six years ago, his wife calls me and tells me that he is dead from an overdose. She wanted me to dress up military. I told her I had thrown that stuff away.

They had a military funeral for him. I didn't tell her that he had told me earlier that he didn't want to be buried with military honors. I guess he knew it was coming.

After you come back, I guess the hardest part was trying to adjust to being home. I couldn't sleep at night and I'd try to sleep during the day. I was still on drugs, but after a bit I started slacking off because I knew I wasn't going anywhere. My folks knew that when I came home that I was, well, doped up. They'd find dope in my pockets and flush it down the toilet. My mom told me I didn't come back the way I left.

My mom and grandmother made a promise to the Virgin of Guadalupe that they would make a trip to Mexico City if I came back alive. I didn't even know about it and I wasn't ready to go. I didn't even enjoy myself. My grandmother went from the front of the cathedral to the altar on her knees. I myself couldn't see it, I guess, because I don't believe in things like that. At that time, I wasn't old enough to vote yet, but I was old enough to die for my country. So, up to this day, I don't even vote, I can't see it.

I had promised myself that when I came back I wasn't going to work for a year. I went to the unemployment office and those people wanted to put me to work. I told them to shove it. I said, "Hey man, the government says I'm entitled to some unemployment." When you come back you're hard to get along with, your attitude is completely different from when you left. I had some money saved up, so I wasn't worried about it.

DAVID'S BROTHER

Freddie Delgado
Infantryman 9th Mechanized Unit
101st Airborne
April 1970 to March 1971

I was in the 9th Mechanized Unit. I was there a few months and then they had this deal about de-escalating. They told me that if I had more than six months in country, I could go home with the colors. I needed one more month in country in order to get sent home. Instead, I was sent to the 101st Airborne.

The army was a weird trip. They spent thousands of dollars to train you in some sort of specialized area, then they put you in something else. When I got to Viet Nam, they put me in a mechanized infantry unit. At Fort Knox, Kentucky, I was trained to be in a tank unit.

I remember I turned twenty-one crossing into Cambodia in May of 1970. There was no boundary line, but you could tell the difference in terrain. When we went over there, we found a lot of bunkers and caches. I was an M-60 machine gunner. All I had on my mind was how I was going to keep my ass alive and go back home.

167

My brother David had already gone to Viet Nam, and when he came out I was going over there. He went through a lot of combat. He was in the Big Red One. He told me more or less what to expect. So I sort of went on his little code. It sort of saved me. He told me that when you get into a fire fight, don't freak out. Get yourself some cover and fire back to keep those fuckers down. He got wounded over there just like I did.

The first month I was there, I was wounded in an ambush out in Cambodia. I knew it was going to come down because we used the same fucking trail every fucking day. We'd cross into Cambodia from Viet Nam and go back and forth. We'd been up all night in an ambush in Cambodian territory, and we were returning to Viet Nam early in the morning. Luckily, I was between two *vatos* on top of a track. I was dozing off when I felt the track slowing down. All of a sudden, two RPG's hit a tank and there was a lot of smoke. A few seconds later I heard guys screaming to my side. I didn't get hit bad because I was sort of leaning to the side and dozing off when the shrapnel hit. I jumped off the track and looked for cover. That's when I realized I had been hit. What happened was that the VC had used some civilians as decoys. They made some civilians cross the road in order to slow down the convoy to make it an easy target.

I got hit on one of the big veins of my shoulder. I knew I was hit when I felt a little dizzy and it knocked me out a little bit. I looked around and called for the medic. Half of it looked like it was blown away, but it wasn't that bad. I saw the medic, he was pinned down and crying. Sonofabitch, I had to go to him instead of him going to me. The fucking captain saw me and told me, "Delgado! Where are you going?" I was crawling to the medic and then he got freaked out. He didn't question me no more. He probably thought I was booking it, or something.

It took me about a week to recover from my wound. The wound left me with sort of a grudge, and it made me pissed off.

I thought to myself, when I get back to the unit I'm really going to try and kill people—to get even. When I finally got to my unit, I talked to one of the guys and I asked him for Gonzales. He told me that he had gotten killed. I couldn't believe it. I had barely been gone a week and he got killed. When I heard about it, the John Wayne in me went away.

Ken Weatherby, I think his name was, this is about ten years ago so it's hard to remember names, and me were in the same unit, the ninth, and he got shipped to the 11th Cav. I had given him my address so we could keep in touch. I wrote to him, and they sent me a letter back saying that he was killed. He only had a week or so to go in Nam. That tripped me out. I didn't believe it. He was a nice quiet *vato*—*gabacho*—quiet like me, and he kept his own head together.

When we got hit over there in Cambodia, we called radio *y de volada,* before you knew it, they had the jets. When they left, the cobra was combing the area, spraying the whole area with rockets and mini-guns. Everything was like nothing could survive in there. They didn't find nothing, *eh,* when they went to look for body count. I was about the third man back, with the sixty machine gun. That motherfucker is heavy, when you walk in the mud, it sucks you in. Plus the ammo, I swear to God, I think if we had an ambush I don't think the fucker would've worked because it was all full of mud.

It was a peaceful land over there in Cambodia. The country was real pretty. In the valleys, I swear to God, the trees had flowers around them, it looked real nice. I said to myself, "Such a pretty country, but it will fuck you up. You don't know who in the hell is going to do it to you, eh."

We were almost trapped, you know, like pinned down. We went into a place where there were little rivers and tides. We went into this place and the tide was in and we're supposed to come back before dark, before the tide goes back out. We stayed there so long that the boats couldn't get to us because the water wasn't there. So we had to go through fucking mud, *y la chingada.* We had some scouts, some converted VC's. They were rapping to us and telling us that the VC were right behind us because they could more or less tell. I sort of depended on those *vatos*. I trusted those guys a little bit because one time we were walking on this fucking rice paddy dike. We had these scouts, and we had two different trails to go and this *vato* decided he had a choice. He looked around and he knew all of the booby trap trips. He had to go one way and decided to go the other way. If he had been a traitor, he would have told us guys to go one way. But he didn't, so he was a cool dude. One of the things I regret is not taking many pictures over there. My *camaradas* took pictures of me and they took them home. I was out in the bush and I didn't want to carry a little camera with me.

I actually only got into a few fire fights. The thing about being in the jungle and not knowing what was going to hit you was the scariest thing to me. I remember one time it was raining at night full blast. All I had was a poncho to cover myself with. I was so tired that I fell asleep but any little noise would wake me up. I sort of aged over there a little bit.

As I mentioned earlier, after the Ninth was sent home, I was transferred to the 101st airborne. That was a trip. You know, you hear stories about the 101st and how tough they were. Camp Eagle was the headquarters of the 101st. It was over there by Hue. There they had rangers, Green Berets, police dogs and a lot of other stuff. I was sent to the 2/17th, it was an airmobile unit. I had a lot of experiences over there. I would think about the *vatos* here in Corcoran, the same age as me, and not going through this experience. I would wonder if they would believe the experience. I don't think the 101st was any tougher than the ninth, just different terrain. You are fighting the same *vatos*. The rangers used to go on ambushes with six men teams. They'd get their asses blown away. They used to come back *todos para la chingada,* all mosquito bitten.

There were a lot more Chicanos in the 101st than there were in the Ninth. I got to know a lot of the *vatos* at Camp

Eagle. The head cook and head mailman were Chicanos. I also had a *camarada* who was a chopper pilot. Most of these guys were from the Rio Grande Valley in Texas, *"El Valle."* Everything turned out right in the 101st. It was beautiful. I wasn't out in the field as much as when I was with the Ninth. The first month or two I was out in the field, then they got me a better job. I drove a truck for a while and stayed close to the base camp. I didn't have to go on any more combat missions. It was good for me, I liked that better.

I think one thing that helped me was always being alert. One time we were walking on this dike and three *vatos* who were in front of me passed right over a booby trap. But I was a little more aware of the greenery around the booby trap. One spot was more like a dry area; it looked kind of odd to me. I stopped and looked at it and it had a little piece of metal pointing up. I stopped the squad behind me and said, "I think there's a booby trap here." We blew it up with some plastic explosives. Three *vatos* passed by the booby trap. Lucky they didn't step on it. They should have been more *trucha.* But you're tired, *eh,* everyday you're humping, you get tired.

In Viet Nam, it seemed to me that everybody put out 100%. People like truck drivers and helicopter door gunners were many times under fire. Almost everybody in the army there worked a lot of hours. But it was different being out in the field. At least the door gunners and truck drivers would sleep in nice clean beds. They would have a hot dinner and maybe a couple of cold beers. But out in the bush, we didn't have any of that. I would be in my dirty clothes and muddy boots, and then I would see the door gunners with nice green uniforms and shiny black boots. When I was in the Ninth, I carried the M-60 and that's what the door gunners got but they are converted differently, they don't have a stock on them. So when I got to the 101st, I wanted to be sent to the door gunners school. I wanted to be a door gunner. I didn't want to be a grunt no more. I thought the door gunners had a better life. Being an experienced M-60 gunner, I thought I'd get into the school quick. I applied and they didn't even pick me. It was *gabachos* that had that job. It was risky, but I think it was a lot better than being a grunt.

I felt good and I felt sad when I was leaving for home because I was leaving a lot of good buddies. I felt bad leaving them behind. The night before I left we threw a big party. I looked back to the first month I was there and you see all of the guys who are going home and you think to yourself, "I wish it was me." Then it was my turn to get out, and I thought I had done my time. It felt good to be out.

I remember before I left the Oakland Army depot that there were *vatos* who were just back from Nam. The guys who came back from Viet Nam are served a steak dinner. I got picked for KP even though I was going to Viet Nam. I was there doing KP in the dining hall when someone told me, "You going to Viet Nam?" I said, "Yep." He said, "Well, good luck, take care of yourself." Then he left. When I was coming back from Viet Nam, I was eating a steak and this new guy at the door told me, "You going to Viet Nam?" I said, "No, are you going over there, *ese?*" Then I told the *vato,* "Take care." I tripped out because I was in the same position a year ago. I extended a couple of weeks in Nam in order to get an early out from the Army.

They discharged me from the Army at Fort Lewis, Washington. They gave me my papers saying, "You, as of now, are a free man." We got there about midnight and they paid us about three in the morning. When I left Fort Lewis, I had six hundred dollars in my pocket.

The first thing I experienced when I got back to the world was that people looked more healthy, more *gordos,* and they weren't as small. I said to myself, "Boy, are they feeding you people right over here." There was an incident that happened at my sister's house. We were watching TV when I got up to change the station and at the same time a jet plane was flying over and made a sonic boom. It rattled the windows and shit. I hit the ground automatically and when I got up, I felt embarrassed. My sister and my little brother didn't think it was funny. They realized what was happening to me. After a little bit we started to laugh it off.

One time I was asleep and my dad was sleeping there in the same room, when all of a sudden, I gave a big old grunt. My father told me, *"Estas aqui, ya no estas alla."* That happened the first night I was there. I woke up relieved. I got used to it fast. There was a time people were really talking about the Viet Nam War, but I didn't talk about it. Even if I would have told them what happened, they wouldn't have believed me. So, I decided not to say anything about it when people would ask me questions about Viet Nam.

When I came home, I saw some guys with long hair and I was pissed off at them because they didn't go where I went. I guess most of the guys were caught in the middle of the war because we were drafted. After I was home for a few months, I let my hair grow long.

When I went to get my physical for the army, me and Gary Good were the only ones from Corcoran going to Fresno to take the physical. Gary had some reds, and asked me if I wanted some to pump my blood pressure up. I told him, "Naw, I'll take my chances." By the time they took his pressure, he was already fucked up. They read his meter and they said, "Naw, this guy took something. You're coming back next week, *cabron.*" I don't know what happened the next week, but I guess he used a different technique because Gary never went into the army. Every time I looked at him, I would say to myself, "I know something about you, fucker."

I couldn't land a job when I got back, and don't know why. The job I did get was working with my dad at Boswell Land Company on a seasonal basis.

SALT AND PEPPER

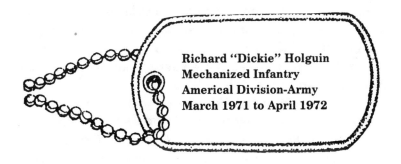

Richard "Dickie" Holguin
Mechanized Infantry
Americal Division-Army
March 1971 to April 1972

H is name was Captain Bud, but I used to call him, "Captain Dud" to his face. I got busted because I refused a direct order from him. He was a dud and he got some people killed before. He called a mortar strike on top of some South Vietnamese soldiers. I had shown him there on the map, "Hey, there's friendlies right there." "No," he said, "You're not reading the map right." "No," I told him, "You're not reading the fucking map right." He called the mortars on them and killed three or four South Vietnamese soldiers. He tried to put the blame on our mortar crew by saying that they didn't use the right grid coordinates. Three other times he called in the wrong coordinates for our position to the people on the hill, and they fired artillery at us. That's not cool. The reason I got busted by Captain Bud was because I refused to take my track down a certain way. I had been down that road before and it was too dangerous.

I was sitting down and I had just finished writing a letter.

175

I wrote. "There is nothing really goiong on right now, sweetheart, just kicking back." Everybody was writing letters home. I wrote SWAK and folded the envelope when all of a sudden some RPG rockets were fired at us. I looked to the side and saw the lieutenant's track get hit with a RPG rocket. His track was obvious because of the three antennas on the track. I saw the lieutenant sitting and burning at the same time. They got him good. Immediately we began returning the fire. It wasn't like another time when some of the new guys had jumped off the track and didn't fire back. I had gotten on their cases for doing that. They accused me of being gung ho. But I told them that they were fucking up because if they didn't return the fire and keep those guys off our asses we could wind up dead.

Our guys to the left forgot that we had some men out front setting up booby-traps. We had South Vietnamese soldiers out there taking a bath. I knew that, I didn't give a fuck because they were South Vietnamese. They weren't American. When the firing stopped, someone said, "Hey, so and so is out there." "Where?" we asked. "Out there setting booby-traps," they replied. "Well, you guys are going to have to get them." There was two guys out there, one was dead and one was wounded. The guy who got killed made a mistake by trying to run back to the perimeter. Whoever killed that GI knew it because I heard someone say he shot at a gook that was running. It was the GI. The other guy made it because he was laying down. He later told us he made an indentation in the ground because he was hugging it that close. When the South Vietnamese came in, they were talking all kinds of shit. They were probably calling us all kinds of names. The South Vietnamese soldiers were a bunch of assholes, a bunch of ignorant son-of-a-bitches who didn't know what the hell they were doing. The ones I thought a lot about were the Korean Marines. They were some bad son-of-a-bitches, I seen them bust heads.

We went on a mission one time and I saw Salt and

Pepper. Salt and Pepper were these two American Marines, one black and the other white, who had turned traitor and went to the Viet Cong side. I had seen both of them with my own eyes. We were going by this open area close to pineapple forest. I was looking around with my binoculars and saw six gooks with black pajamas on, a white dude and a *mayate*. I told Larry, my track commander at the time, and he saw them too.

We called the LT. He said, "You guys are fucking crazy. Ain't nothing out there." I said, "Hey, let me open up man, the son-of-a-bitches are out there." What they did was smart because they were walking the shadow of the jungle. It was hard to see them. For some reason I just happened to look that way, and I kept staring and staring, until I saw them. Larry Pence saw them, too. They wouldn't let us open up on them. The Viet Cong even stopped and looked at us. One of them was a white son-of-a-bitch, blond hair, and the *mayate*, blacker than black. So we continued going until we hit some mines. The South Vietnamese soldiers who were walking behind us were the ones who hit them, so we had to stop.

As we were waiting for them to clear everything up, we saw this archway along the edge of the jungle. I said, "Larry, check that out, man. Look at that archway." He said, "That's weird out here in the jungle." It was like a doorway cut with vines wrapped around real neat. I said, "As lazy as I am, I would walk through that archway instead of cutting my way through the vines." Sure enough, here comes this South Vietnamese Lieutenant and walks through the archway. As he went through, I swear he went about ten feet in the fucking air, just like a rag doll. I said to myself, that probably could have been me if I had been walking the goddammed ground because I would have taken the shortcut. Then I thought again, and I don't think I would have done that.

A bit after that, we received some sniper fire from a village. We killed everything from the chickens on up.

I stayed out in the jungle until the day before I left. I

didn't want to go to the rear because there were too many hassles. There were a lot of junkies. It was just a big hassle. You got in fights a lot. The REMFs would act real smart, and you weren't ready for no bullshit. They used to extend a lot of our missions because we would fight too much. One time, some of the Chicanos from LA got into a fire fight with some *gabachos*. Nobody was hit, but they came pretty close. Those Chicanos from the City were different from the small town Chicanos. So, I decided to stay out in the field until I got ready to leave. Fuck it, if I'm going to die, I'm going to die.

I went to look for Pedro Gomez from Corco once. I had his unit location so I decided to visit him one time I was in the rear. When I got to his company, he wasn't there. I asked around and one guy told me he was out pimping some Vietnamese chicks.

I had a buddy, Joe Martinez. He had forty-five days to go when he got himself blowed up, blew one of his legs off, broke the other leg in about 3 places, broke an arm, punctured a lung, cut him up all to hell. When he hit that boobytrap, it shook me up because we were pretty close. He was souvenir hunting when he got hit. I used to tell those guys, use a grappling hook with the rope, throw it over there and then drag it towards you. If it don't blow up, then you can keep it. When I used to leave my bodies (dead enemy) laying around, I used to always put grenades underneath the suckers. If Charlie wanted to pick up his bodies, I'll leave his little fucking-ass a present. When I set boobytraps up, I always boobytrapped my boobytrap. The same guy who set the boobytrap was the same guy who picked it up, too. You always got to check out your boobytrap because Charlie will put a boobytrap on your boobytrap, and that son-of-a-bitch will watch your ass.

When I was in the Da Nang processing center getting ready to go home, I heard someone call my name and looked at the guy. It was one of the Chicanos who was on the plane when I came over. He asked, me, *"Que paso con so y so?"* I don't know. *"Quien sabe,"* I answered. All of a sudden we looked over to the side and there was another guy that came on the plane with us. Out of about ten Chicanos that I got to know on the plane over there, only one of us didn't come back. He was a confirmed dead man because one of the guys that was in his unit saw him get killed. The rest all came back on the bird.

When I got home I had to adjust to the idea of having a family because I had gotten married and had a daughter by the time I got out of the army. I did a lot of things I shouldn't have done and I didn't give a fuck. For a long time I didn't give a fuck. I still don't, but to a certain point, I'm a little bit different. I'm still adjusting, Some days I get up and just get in the car and take off. I have to have that time to be alone and to keep my head from exploding.

I've told my wife and other people about some of the dreams I have had and they don't believe me. I dreamed that I was fighting this war with these certain people, when I was in the seventh grade before I had even heard of Viet Nam. One day when I was in Viet Nam, I just stopped right there and said, "Wait a minute, I've been here, I know I've been here before because everything is too familiar." I started thinking back. Hey, I had a dream back in the 7th grade I was doing the same thing I am doing now. It was like being reincarnated.

TRANSLATIONS

1. Ah la madre - Oh Shit
2. Asina - Like that
3. Cabrón - literally billygoat; asshole
4. Cábula- Bullshit or jive
5. Camarada - Comrade
6. Carnal - Brother
7. Chingazos - Blows or to fight
8. Cuero - Skin
9. De a mádre - Like mad
10. En chinga - Like mad
11. Ese - You
12. Escamado - Afraid
13. Estaba cabrón allí el pedo - It was a very hazardous place
14. Estás aquí, ya no estás allá. - You are here now, not over there.
15. Están cabrones estos vatos aqui - These guys are tough
16. Gabacho - A white man
17. Gordos - Fat
18. Gringo - A white man
19. Hijola - Golly; hell
20. Jefita - Mother
21. Jefito - Father
22. Iba a la bara-me ponía pedo-y a tirar chingazos - I would go to bar to get drunk and get into fights
23. Loco - Crazy

24. Más coraje que la chingada - I would get very angry
25. Mayate - A black man
26. Marijuano - A smoker of marijuana
27. Mensos - Dummies
28. Me pongo muy indio - I get like an Indian
29. Mi dieron en la madre - That knocked the hell out of me
30. Negros - Blacks
31. No más - No more
32. Orale, aquí estábamos hablando español y la chingada. Habia tres indio y tres Chicanos - We all spoke Spanish. There were three Indians and three Chicanos
33. Orale cabrón - O.K. punk
34. Orale ése - Hey you
35. Para tirar chingazos - To fight; throw blows
36. Porque - Because
37. . . . porque estaba muy chavalon y me importaba pito - . . . because I was so young and I didn't give a damn
38. Qué pasó con so y so - What happened to so and so
39. Raza - Chicanos
40. Rucas - Women
41. Se llamaba - His name was
42. Susto - Fright
43. Te chingaste, baboso - You got screwed stupid
44. Todos para la chingada - All messed up
45. Todos pelones, todos hasta la chingada - Baldheaded and all messed up
46. Trucha - Be alert
47. Vato - Dude, guy
48. Vatos locos - Crazy guys
49. Verga - Penis
50. Y a toda madre - And everything was great
51. Y de volada - And they came
52. Y la chingada - And bullshit like that
53. Yo no voy escribir hasta que no me escriban - I am not going to write until they write me.

GLOSSARY

AIT: Advanced Infantry Training.

AK-47: Assault rifle used by the North Vietnamese and Viet Cong.

APC: Armored Personnel Carrier.

ARVN: Army of the Republic of South Viet Nam or a soldier of this army.

AWOL: Absent Without Leave.

Basic: Basic training.

Battalion: Four or five companies of infantry.

Beaucoup: French for many.

Big Red One: First Infantry Division

Body Count: The counting of enemy dead.

Boonies or Bush: The jungle or the field.

Cav: Cavalry.

Cherry: A new soldier.

Chieu Boi: Program designed to provide amnesty for communist soldiers.

Chinnok: Large transport helicopter.

Chopper: Helicopter.

Claymore Mine: Antipersonnel mine.

CO: Commanding Officer.

Cobra: Helicopter gunship.

Company: Four platoons with approximately 100 to 150 men.

Connex Box: Large metal container used to transport materials by helicopter.

Corpsman: Navy medic.

Didi or Didi Mau: Vietnamese for "get out" or "leave."

DMZ: Demilitarized Zone at the 17th parallel.

Duece-and-a Half: Two ton transport truck.

Dust-Off: Medical evacuation by helicopter.

EM: Enlisted Man.

Fire Fight: Small arms engagement.

First Cav: First Cavalry Division

Free Fire Zone: Large tracts of land occupied by the communist where the US military could fire freely.

Fragging: When fragmentation grenades were used to wound or kill NCO's or officers.

G.I.: Government Issue. Applied to army personnel.

Gook: Pejorative for Vietnamese. Other terms; dinks, slants, zipper-heads.

Hootch: Makeshift dwelling.

Howitzer: A short cannon that shoots shells at a high angle of fire. Standard US cannons were 105mm, 155mm, and 175mm.

Hump: To walk in the jungle, especially with a heavy load.

Incoming: Mortar or artillery landing on a position.

In Country: Viet Nam.

Jarheads: Marines.

Kit Carson Scout: Former Viet Cong soldier used as scouts by the US military.

K.P.: Kitchen Police-mess duty.

LBJ: Long Binh Jail. Largest military stockade in Viet-Nam.

Lifers: Career Soldier. Many times disliked by conscripts and noncareer soldiers.

LP: Listening Post. Two or three soldiers sent outside a night perimeter for observation.

LZ: Landing zones for helicopters.

MACV: Military Assistance Command, Viet Nam.

Mama-San: Vietnamese Woman.

Medevac: Medical evacuation.

M-79: Single barrel grenade launcher.

MIA: Missing In Action:

M-16: Standard US rifle used after 1966.

M-60: Machine Gun: The weapon with the most firepower in an infantry platoon or company.

Monsoon: The rainy season.

Montagnards: Native mountain people of Viet Nam. Culturally and ethnically distinct from Vietnamese.

MP's: Military Police.

NCO: Noncommissioned Officer.

NVA: North Vietnamese Army.

Piaster: South Vietnamese money.

Platoon: Approximately 35 to 45 men.

Pointman or Point: The first man in a file of infantry.

Rabbit: Black slang for white person.

Rear or Rear Area: A military installation that is relatively secure in contrast to the jungle.

Reconn: Reconnaissance.

REMF: Rear Echelon Motherfucker

RPG: Rocket Propelled Grenade.

R&R: Rest and Recuperation. One week vacations given to soldiers.

RTO: Radiotelephone Operator-radioman.

Short or Getting Short: A soldier approaching the end of his Viet Nam tour.

Standdown: A short rest from the field in a rear area.

Stars & Stripes: US military newspaper.

Steel Pot: A soldier's helmet.

Stockade: A military prison.

SWAK: Sealed With A Kiss.

TET: Vietnamese lunar new year.

TDY: Temporary Duty.

The World: The United States.

Tracks: Tracked vehicles.

VC: Viet Cong.

Order Form

Chusma House Publications
P.O. Box 467
San Jose, CA 95103-0467

(408) 947- 0958

I would like to order _____ copy(s) of *SOLDADOS: CHICANOS IN VIET NAM*.

I am enclosing a check or money order in the amount of $_____, payable to Chusma House Publications.
($11.95 plus $2.45 shipping and handling, $1.75 shipping and handling for each additional book ordered)

Name _____

Address _____

City _____ State _____ Zip _____

(Allow three to four weeks for delivery)

About The Author

Charley Trujillo is an instructor in the Intercultural/ International Studies Division at De Anza College in Cupertino, California. He is a native of Corcoran, California, a small agricultural community in the San Joaquin Valley of California. He served in Viet Nam as an infantry sergeant and was awarded a Purple Heart and Bronze Star Medal. After his discharge he received a B.A. from U.C. Berkeley and an M.A. from San Jose State University.